Discover Psychic Tarot Reading, Tarot Card Meanings, Numerology, Astrology and Reveal What The Universe Has In Store for You

CLAIM THIS NOW

Discover the Ancient Healing Power of Reiki, Awaken Your Mind, Body, Spirit and Heal Your Life

Reiki has the power to heal our minds, bodies, and spirits in ways few of us can imagine.

This is applicable to individuals of any age with physical, mental, emotional, or even spiritual problems.

For many years Reiki has been a highly guarded secret but it is intelligent energy, which automatically goes to where it is needed.

Find out more in this complete guide to an ancient healing art to living a happier, healthier, and better life.

A SPIRITUAL START!

Start your week with gratitude, joy, inspiration, and love.

Healing, motivation, inspiration, challenge and guidance straight to your inbox every week!

FIND OUT MORE

TABLE OF CONTENTS

Introduction

What is Tarot?

A brief history of Tarot Reading

CHAPTER ONE: How Does Tarot Work?

CHAPTER TWO: The most common tarot card spreads

Most Common Tarot Layouts or Spreads

The True Love Layout

The Success Layout

The Celtic - Cross Layout

CHAPTER THREE: A Guide To Your Tarot Deck

The Major Arcana

The Minor Arcana

CHAPTER FOUR: How to Use Your Tarot Cards

CHAPTER FIVE: Card Combinations, Patterns and Elemental Dignities

Similar Meanings

Elemental Dignities

Qualities of Elements

Elemental Dignities and its Relationships

CHAPTER SIX: Card Placements within a Tarot Spread

Reading Cards in Tarot Spread Position

Three Card Spreads

CHAPTER SEVEN: Card Reversals and Timing

Card Reversals

Timing in Tarot Cards

Cards Denoting Transition or New Beginnings

Relationship Cards

CHAPTER EIGHT: The Meaning of Each Tarot Card

The Major and Minor Arcana

Court Cards

CHAPTER NINE: Reading a Tarot Card for the Day

CHAPTER TEN: Tarot as a Spiritual Doorway

A Cosmic String around Your Finger

Draw a Card and Cast a Spell

Om and Amen

CHAPTER ELEVEN: Bringing All Your Mystic Skills Together to Get the Results That You Want

CHAPTER TWELVE: Setting boundaries

CHAPTER THIRTEEN: Tarot Reading FAQ

CHAPTER FOURTEEN: Tarot Myths Busted

CHAPTER FIFTEEN: Summary…

Using Narratives or Storytelling in Tarot Reading

Shuffling Your Cards

Conclusion

INTRODUCTION

What is Tarot?

The Tarot consists of a deck of 78 cards that, over the centuries, absorbed the knowledge, stories, beliefs, histories, morals and life lessons of numerous cultures. Combine that with the all-powerful mind we possess, and we can use the Tarot to obtain vision into our lives, allow us to achieve, and strengthen us when we need to cope. Know that when reading the Tarot, we already know the answers to our own questions. However, those answers are concealed within our subconscious. The Tarot assists us in extracting that information.

There are 3 predominant tarot card systems which are generally used today - Marseille (around 1440), Rider-Waite-Smith (around 1909), and Thoth (around 1969). I personally like Rider-Waite-Smith and lean towards the Golden Dawn interpretive method.

Others may tell you that you don't need to know anything to read tarot. They say you can simply use your "psychic intuition." I humbly disagree. Critical theory is vital to accurately gaining a complete understanding of the Tarot.

A brief history of Tarot Reading

Tarot cards are said to have originated from Italy in the early 15th century. It was originally comprised of 21 trump cards and was created as a game for the nobles. Friars and conservative nobles during the era called the tarot cards as demonic cards because it contained characters or images that pertain to demons and death.

In the late 18th century, a cartomancer known as "Etielle" published a book containing the meaning of the cards and how they can affect the spirituality, destiny, and personality of a person. However, his version of tarot cards only contained 32 cards.

During the 19th century, Eliphas Levi correlated the tarot cards with the Hebrew Kabbalah. The new deck of tarot cards was comprised of 78 cards. Eliphas introduced the new deck as mystery cards that can answer every question of life. Since then, this new deck became the basic cards for a tarot reading.

Since the early tarot readers were almost precise on their readings and guidance, many believed that the cards could foretell a future event. Hence, until this day, many people still turn to tarot reading for guidance in their businesses, relationship, health, and decisions.

Chapter One
How Does Tarot Work?

Of course, the first question that many people ask is: Does a tarot reading really work? As explained above, not every reading works every time, but in general, both active readers and their subjects get a lot out of the process. It can be the subject of a long debate in another book if these tarot readings work because of the intuition of the reader or because of the tarot cards actually provide a connection to a universal store of knowledge and energy.

The concept of synchronicity seems to be what powers the tarot. Even though this term has gotten used in popular culture, a famous doctor of psychology first described it, and this doctor's name was Carl Jung. This is simply defined as two or even more events that appear to be related to each other but do not appear to have a link between why they happened.

In other words, events can be joined by meaning as well as by causality. When describing this concept back in the 1920s, Carl Jung said that there were no coincidences, and that is close to what tarot scholars believe. It is similar to somebody shrugging their shoulders at a series of unlikely events that seem related and saying, Stuff just happens.

This explains what happens when a particular way and unique way of shuffling the deck produces each card that fits into the pattern. It is also what happens when all of the cards merge together into an entire pattern. Practitioners believe that the phenomenon of synchronicity creates exactly the right spread of tarot cards to produce the appropriate pattern of symbols and meanings that answer the questions presented to the deck. Are the questions asked of the deck, the tarot card reader, the universe as a whole or the subject herself? That is for each individual who studies the tarot to decide.

In other words, the graphical symbols, card numbers, and their inherent meanings reflect the powerful minds of the readers and the subjects. This language of symbols, the language that the cards speak can talk to the minds of the reader and subject in a way that words cannot.

It is not hard to speculate that the ability to understand symbols is even older than the ability to understand words. Probably, the first words were actually symbols. It is certainly true that the oldest known languages in the world were written down with images instead of phonetic letters.

People are able to grasp the inner meaning of the symbols that represent their meanings in words. By doing this, they learn to understand what the deck is trying to tell them truly. In fact, the deck is probably just a pile of cardboard. That is like saying the Declaration of Independence is just a piece of old paper. It is the meaning that human minds can take away from the symbols on the cards that makes them work so well.

Interpretation Of Symbols In Occult Tarot

Each card has a symbol and charts that diagram some general ways to interpret them. However, the real interpretation comes from the reader, and each one is unique. Cards may be interpreted on their own, by their position in the spread, and also through the filter of the reader's own experiences.

This means that each reading is unique. Also, two readers might interpret the same patterns and symbols in different ways. Does this mean that one of them is wrong? As mentioned above, there are failed readings. However, these are actually very rare. It is more likely that both readers have different perspectives about the issues, and they may each receive somewhat different images because of this.

If one person says a glass is half full and another says the class is half empty, does that mean

That one is wrong? No, each of these people is simply expressing a different general outlook on the same glass with the same amount of liquid in it. In this same way, two readers may give different readings, and both be right.

Again, the future is not immutable. The subject usually has great control over the outcome, and the cards may get proven wrong. Hopefully, this is because the subject received great insight from reading and learned to approach some situation or challenge in her life in a more positive way. If the tarot contributed to this, but the reading did not actually foretell the future, does this make the tarot wrong? No, the tarot worked exactly the way it was intended to.

The final concept from this section is based upon reminding readers that the tarot is only a deck of cards. Some may be plain, and some may be very beautiful. Skilled artists craft some decks, but others are made at home. Either way, the outcome of reading doesn't really say much about a pile of cards. It says something about the reader, but it says more about the subject who approaches the tarot for answers to important questions.

There are plenty of instruction guides to help readers learn to use tarot cards. Volumes have been written. Simple guides to meaning can be found in books or even on the Internet. But these instruction guides are all meaningless on their own without the talent and intuition of the reader and the cooperative insight of the questioner.

Mainly, the tarot is not an instruction guide. It doesn't provide a fix-it guide for people with problems. However, it is intended to provide insight into problems, how these problems arose, and possibly, how to avoid the worst consequences of them in the future.

Chapter Two
The most common tarot card spreads.

In this chapter, you'll learn the most common tarot spreads or layouts for beginners and also for expert tarot readers. Be reminded though that this is listed in no particular order. You'll also get to learn the meaning of each spread so you can easily connect the cards and be able to answer your client's question more accurately. It's up to you to determine which spread might work best for any type of reading; it's probably best to learn them all so you can have the chance to see what's more appropriate for you and your subjects. Now, let's lay down the cards on the table!

Most Common Tarot Layouts or Spreads

The True Love Layout

This spread or layout focuses on a person's relationship, but not just about one's romantic relationship (although it's the most common topic among seekers). It's also used to evaluate a person's physical, spiritual, and emotional connection to their current or potential partners. It's a six card spread, and the pattern signifies a certain interpretation.

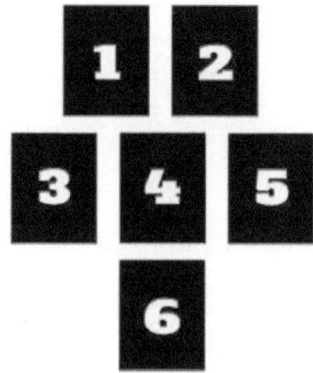

#1 Card: Signifies how the seeker feels about the current relationship that he/she is in. It also includes one's outlook towards the relationship.

#2 Card: Signifies the seeker's partner (either spouse, boyfriend/girlfriend) and his/her feelings about the relationship as well as one's expectations

#3 Card: Represents the connection or common characteristics of the seeker and his/her partner

#4 Card: Represents the qualities of strength in the relationship

#5 Card: Represents the weakness qualities of the relationship and the things both parties should improve on

#6: Represents how the relationship is going to go or what needs to be done to maintain or perhaps create a more meaningful connection with one another.

The Success Layout

Obviously, this type of spread is concern about an individual's successes in terms of career, dreams, or even in oneself. This kind of layout will also help a person in how to overcome certain challenges and could also get some advice on how to achieve a resolution to a problem. It may also represent the things an individual already has like the resources or skills that are available. It's also a five – card spread with this layout:

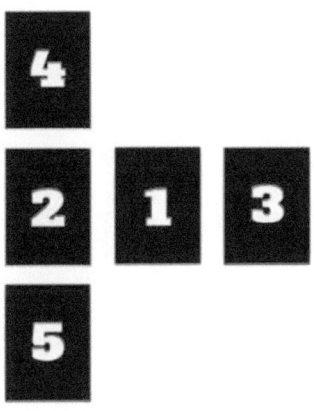

#1 Card: Represents the main challenge or problem of the seeker

#2 Card: Represents the complications from those challenges

#3 Card: Denotes some factors that the seeker needs to know which are affecting the current situation

#4 Card: Signifies the people or ideas that could make the seeker grow to achieve a certain goal

#5 Card: Indicates what the seeker needs to do to achieve a goal, avoid failure as much as possible, and become successful in an endeavor.

The Celtic - Cross Layout

The Celtic – Cross spread is one of the most complex types of tarot reading but it's perhaps one of the most original layouts, and it has been used for many centuries. The layout's versatility has been helpful in assessing complicated queries because it can be read in different ways depending on the card's combinations and patterns. This kind of layout basically focuses on the seeker's issues as well as the outside factors that are at play. This type of layout may be quite hard to understand, especially for beginners, but of course, practice can make you better. This is a 10 – card spread with this layout:

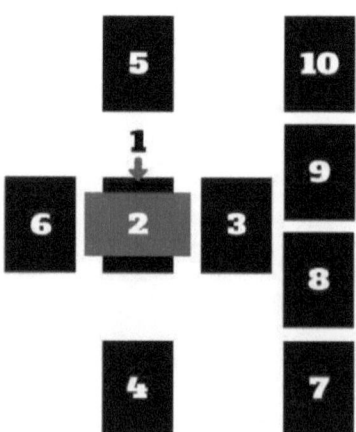

#1 Card: Represents the seeker's current situation

#2 Card: It represents what's holding a person back or what is helping him/her

#3 Card: Focuses more on the seeker's true desire that he/she may be unaware of, as well as the subconscious influences that ultimately affects his/her life

#4 Card: Represents the past events and issues that are still bothering the seeker

#5 Card: Focuses on one's conscious desires and the goals that are very important for the seeker. It can also tell where the person should place his/her energy and how one should use that energy to accomplish an objective.

#6 Card: Represents one's path – either positive or negative. If it's particularly negative, the card in this placement can also tell the seeker how he/she can avoid it or bounce back from it.

#7 Card: Represents the seeker's attitude, ideals, and actions

#8 Card: Represents the kind of energy that the seeker gets from the people surrounding him/her and if this energy is helpful or not

#9 Card: Also known as the revelation card; it denotes that there are things that should not be neglected and one must pay attention to such things because it can have a huge impact in the current or possible situations.

#10 Card: This is the final outcome of a situation, and it is also related to the #5 card. It will tell the reader and the seeker if the energy in a particular issue is complementing or conflicting one another.

Chapter Three
A Guide To Your Tarot Deck

In this section, we'll examine all 78 cards that make up a standard Rider-Waite tarot deck. These interpretations are a product of accepted knowledge about the cards, combined with my own experience working with them. Rather than take them as definitions etched in stone, view them as starting points. You don't need to memorize these definitions. In fact, you can even skip this section for now and start working with the cards in section 3.

This section can serve as an aid when you struggle to find meaning with a card. From here, you can develop your own understanding, which no book can supply. The tarot's value lies in connecting it to your own life and consciousness.

The Major Arcana

The 22 cards of the Major Arcana can be viewed as a sequence through life. This has some appeal for its elegance, but it can also be a limitation. We need not feel obligated to respect this classification. What is generally agreed upon is that these cards are universal experiences. Some of them may dominate your personality. Some of them are people and places that show up again and again. Whoever and wherever you are, these cards can be found on any given day.

0: THE FOOL – The Fool stands outside of time and the universe, and so he is symbolized by the number zero. But he is inextricably drawn to time and the world of life. He recognizes the vanity and illusory nature of existence. Is he enjoying the view, or is he about to step over the cliff? From his perspective, seeing the emptiness of all being, it is one and the same. He is ready to travel in any direction. He is the unborn, the infinite, and not yet bound by any laws of physics, psychology, or government.

1: THE MAGICIAN – Like the prime agent of creation, the Magician takes responsibility and acts, directing the flow of events. Creation, as symbolized by the wand he holds high, is his primary method for inducing magic. However, he has the other elements at his disposal at any time. He unites heaven and earth (note his gestures) and is a channel for the energy that flows through him. He is tied to the infinite and the universe itself (note the infinity sign above his head), and his action is an act of surrender to his higher self. Any action he takes works **through** him.

2: THE HIGH PRIESTESS – The most intuitive sense within us, the High Priestess is a repository of everything that religion can only hint at. She is the unspoken space between thoughts. She is pure love and compassion as emanated by the universe.

3: THE EMPRESS – Unlike the High Priestess, the Empress is all that is earthly and motherly. She is nature, motherhood, the feminine, abundance, the harvest, and the most comfortable aspects of this world.

4: THE EMPEROR – The Emperor is the masculine principle. He is action, confidence, firmness, and decisiveness. He can represent conquest, war, or other confrontation. He is seated, however, and if the situation is to his liking, then he remains firm in his position.

5: THE HIEROPHANT – As a religious figure, the Hierophant (unlike the High Priestess) represents the outer layers of spirituality. He is custom, orthodoxy, formality, ceremony, and tradition. He shows up when a formal situation or procedure is required or about to take place. You can try to fight against these traditions if you think they are nonsense, but like the church, they have a lot of staying power. Sometimes it is easier to accept a tradition, and sometimes you must fight it.

6: THE LOVERS – This card deals with attachment to an outcome. The lovers wish to be united, but it is ultimately in the hands of the larger forces of the universe. The feminine principle is more willing to accept this, while the masculine principle is more concerned with itself and its own power of agency.

7: THE CHARIOT – The Chariot is a card that seeks to balance the masculine and feminine principles. It requires to give and take. Equate this card with the yin and yang symbol of Taoism. A strong charioteer can keep the situation under control. This might indicate the need for better management of a situation.

8: STRENGTH – The Strength card is about using your higher mental faculties to control your lower instincts. These urges include the seven deadly sins of pride, greed, lust, envy, gluttony, wrath, and sloth. All of these sins come from attachment to the individual ego.

9: THE HERMIT – The Hermit is the wise man. Although we think of hermits as isolated from society, this card often turns up when it is time to go into the world and offer the wisdom you have learned. The Hermit is humble and knows that his light will light the way for others. Light does not

Argue – it simply shines.

10: WHEEL OF FORTUNE – The Wheel is a key moment when the potential for reward is great. It may also lead to adversity, but it is primarily a positive sign, in my experience. The key is giving up attachment to a particular outcome. Often good comes from unexpected directions, and in forms, we hadn't expected.

11: JUSTICE – As you sow, so shall you reap. You get what you pay for. The consequences of your past actions are now experienced, for better or worse. Have you lived with integrity? Have you lived up to your ideals? Few of us do, so this card usually involves atonement or retribution for past acts. However, if you have done well, it can also bode well.

12: THE HANGED MAN – As this man is hung in a torturous position, he has an **aha** moment. This state recalls that of the Fool, outside of the universe. But the Hanged Man is still enmeshed in the physical world and his journey.

Nevertheless, he has awoken to the true nature of his existence and the insubstantial nature of this world.

13: DEATH – Despite the dark image we have of death, this card rarely means a **natural** death. More commonly, it indicates the death of a lifestyle or personality and a chance to be born again. Following on the heels of the Hanged Man, Death is an opportunity to reassess how you've been living. Ironically, it is a moment of new growth. Awareness of death allows you to live truly.

14: TEMPERANCE – With a new paradigm comes new feelings and new experiences. With one foot on land and one foot in the water, the angel of Temperance tries to manage and make sense of these new states. He is still dabbling and not fully immersed, cautiously approaching the newness of the world.

15: THE DEVIL – The Devil is the individual ego and its burning desires. This card is the dark inversion of the Lovers card. Who is enchained by the Devil? Humanity. Our human-level mind, our sexuality, our hunger, and all that we cling to. The man and woman have been enchained by their consciousness. The devil is a sense of lack, absence, emptiness, and division.

16: THE TOWER – The Tower is a great destabilization of life in the material world. Whatever you have constructed in this world may be taken from you in an instant. It may not necessarily occur when this card comes up, but it will happen someday. This card is the moment when you remember the transitory nature of the world. The crisis of this card occurs when the material world is used as the basis for your life. This card says Anything that can be taken from you is not truly yours.

17: THE STAR – The Star is the entryway to dreams, hallucinations, and the unshackling of your spirit from your individual ego. Emotion rules this realm, not logic. It may also indicate an intuitive solution rather than an analytical plan.

18: THE MOON – The Moon is a full immersion into the realm of dreams. The ego is nearly gone at this point. The wolf, scorpion, and even the domesticated dog have surrendered to the larger power of nature and the universe. We all possess this intuitive understanding of life.

19: THE SUN – The Sun is the awakened being. He sees that all life emanates through him as love and that all characters in the universe are united by the light. To become light is to transcend time and exist in a state of bliss.

20: JUDGMENT – Judgment is when you see your own identity as an object. And yet, there is still you to witness it. But all personality is disconnected from the experience – there is only the sense of I AM.

21: THE WORLD – Finally, the World. There is no sense of individual identity separate from what is. There is simply THIS. Time is absent. Space is absent. This might be likened to whatever happened before the Big Bang, or where you were before you were born. From the tiniest subatomic particles to the largest universal scales, everything is encased in a single being. This state is completely alien from day-to-day life… and yet, it is always with us. It cannot leave us, or it wouldn't be the World. From the perspective of the World, there is nothing to be done, nothing that can be done, and nothing to fear (since you are the only person in the room). There is no sense of right or wrong. The universe and all of the time can be viewed as an artifact that hovers like a piece of finished art. Time has become a product of the human brain, from which you are disconnected.

The Minor Arcana

Unlike the Major Arcana, which focus on individual states of consciousness, the Minor Arcana are concerned with specific people, events, situations, modes of intelligence, and external experience.

The four suits correspond to the four major cognitive bits of intelligence: emotional intelligence (cups), creative intelligence (wands), logical intelligence (swords), and sensory intelligence (pentacles).

SWORDS

Swords (along with Wands) seem to separate us from other animals. While some animals can reason and use tools in very basic ways, humans have taken logic and design to a completely different level. Why do humans hold the fate of the Earth in their hands? There are more insects than humans on Earth. There are larger, more powerful animals like elephants and whales. There are faster animals like cheetahs and wolves. But it is our ability to think and the reason that allows humans to dominate planet Earth.

Swords is the suit of logic and organization. Here are some examples of Swords at work:

Using a map.
Looking up how to do something online.
Learning the rules of a game or sport.
Setting an itinerary.
Making an appointment.
Designing a cabinet.
Writing the code for a computer program.
Having a business meeting to review the previous quarter.
Using a tool like a compass or a ruler.
Writing an essay.
Engaging in a debate in a reasoned way (not emotionally arguing).
Following a recipe to make a cake.

Here are my interpretations of the Swords cards:

THE ACE OF SWORDS: The bursting forth of logic, planning, and design. This may come at a moment when you've been immersed in one of the other elements, and now it is time for more effective control. The sheer power of reason and design should not be taken lightly. It can completely alter the course of a life or a society. Because of its power to shape and cut through the other elements, swords often dominates, hence the crown. Surrounding the sword are six of the Hebrew letter **Yod**. This letter is associated with humility. To use the sword of reason without humility is to court disaster. As with all power, if it is based on the individual and desire, it will bring destruction. If it is based on love, the greater good, and harmony, it will bring prosperity.

2 OF SWORDS: The querent is safely protected by a sword in each hand. But she cannot see. Furthermore, she has the sea of emotions behind her, but she cannot experience it in this fearful, guarded state. This is a conservative, reactionary position. It may be safe, but eventually, your arms will tire, and you will grow bored. On the other hand, if you've been experiencing too many emotions, this guarded position might be what you need right now. But it is no way to live your whole life.

3 OF SWORDS: This may be the time to let logic dominate emotion. But whose emotions? If they are yours, are you willing to experience the pain or heartbreak? If it is someone else, be aware that you are choosing logic over love. Are you prepared to live with this?

4 OF SWORDS: Although a member of the swords family, this card is a state of meditation. It may be time to pause as you make plans. Instead, daydreaming and rest may allow the intuitive mind to work. If you try to force logic, it can backfire. Sometimes it's best to rest and put the conscious mind aside. When you return to a challenge, you will handle it better.

5 OF SWORDS: Checkmate! This arrogant fellow has outwitted his peers. He doesn't seem to care about their

feelings. A sword is a great divider. It does not build communities, and although you

May enjoy the victory a sword allows, you will not always be the winner. Remember, those who live by the sword shall die by the sword.

6 OF SWORDS: I call this card, moving on. This may come at a time when your plans have fallen through. This forlorn trio glides over a muted sea of emotion. They have their swords with them, but they serve no purpose here. The swords might even block their view. This is no time for planning. It is a time of recovery. It may be best to leave a situation and regroup at a later time.

7 OF SWORDS: This sneaky fellow is confident he's about to pull a fast one on the people he's left behind. And he just might! After all, look at all the weapons he's got. However, you can only hold two swords at any given time. Unless he has friends to wield those extra swords, what good will they serve? Or perhaps he merely hopes to disarm his foes. Note how he carries the swords by the blades – not the best way to handle a weapon! This could signify a person handling a device, weapon, or plan out of their league. Also, what happens if he trips?

8 OF SWORDS: Logic has fenced this person in. The trickle of water at her feet is the only source of joy. It might be better to follow that emotion to a larger body of water. But first, she needs to break free of her bindings. It might be necessary to use those swords first (logical planning), and then get away

from them. We often can't escape from our situation immediately, and some planning may still be required if we hope to find a more fulfilling situation.

9 OF SWORDS: Are you noticing a theme of despair in the sword cards? This fellow, with all his weapons, is besieged by nightmares in the cold dark. He might use his swords like a ladder to climb his way out, or he could leave them behind altogether. But it's so hard to leave our habits behind, even when they trap us.

10 OF SWORDS: The ultimate ruination of a situation dominated by swords. Your eyes face the emotions that you sought, but you are now pinned down (and perhaps destroyed) by your unerring devotion to logic.

THE PAGE OF SWORDS: The initial stirring of plans. When a sword is first held, its weight and power are incredible. The youth looks around and sees what he might accomplish with the power of a plan.

THE KNIGHT OF SWORDS: Action! With more coordination than any other knight, the knight of swords is a terrific opponent indeed. When he focuses, he can overcome nearly any foe.

THE QUEEN OF SWORDS: The queen has used her sharp mind to cut a strong place for herself in the world. But there is a grayness to her being; her emotions choked out of her. Her place is firm, but she is almost a statue.

THE KING OF SWORDS: The king of swords has disarmed all his opponents and has complete power. His view of the world is elevated, and he has a strong pillar behind him. Anyone wishing to overcome him has their work cut out for themselves. Yet despite all this, he is an emotionally hollow creature who can barely manage a grin.

CUPS

As the carrier of emotional intelligence, cups are all about feelings. Not hot or cold, or physical pain or pleasure, but the more powerful sensation of **emotion**. Like breathing, our emotions happen even if we stop thinking about them. But also like breathing, you can take conscious control of your emotions. Here are some examples of Cups at work:

You feel butterflies as you kiss someone for the first time.

Your investments lose a large amount of money, and you feel like you just got punched in the stomach.

Someone tells a silly joke, and you laugh uncontrollably.

You take a much-needed vacation to Hawaii and feel a sense of bliss as you float in the water.

A sad movie brings you to tears.

You miss your subway train by seconds and feel frustrated.

Eating apple pie reminds you of your grandmother's cooking, and you get a warm, fuzzy feeling.

Your pants fall down, and you blush with embarrassment.

Watching the evening news makes you bitter about the world.

Here are my interpretations of the Cup cards:

THE ACE OF CUPS: Look at the ambiguously left/right hand. Look at the unnatural shape of the water falling from the cup. Water doesn't fall like this! It actually goes **up** before curving down. And the streams are so tightly focused. This card represents an opportunity for emotion, and when emotion comes through, it is not in a general way. It is clearly defined. All emotions are based on the emotion of universal awareness, the seeing into the pure undivided love that is the universe sometimes called **agape**. The material world rests upon the emotions in the form of the lily pads. Peace (in the form of the dove) delivers balance and symmetry to the emotions.

2 OF CUPS: In its most basic differentiation, the universe splits into masculine and feminine principles. The masculine is active. The feminine is passive. But this card typically symbolizes a partner or goal that is unwilling to work with the querent. Do not lust after results, as Aleister Crowley says. This card often comes up when you desire something to happen, but the universe isn't giving it to you. Let go and surrender to the universe.

3 OF CUPS: A harmonious interaction with the parts of the universe. This card looks like a party because it is. When a group of individual emotions is in sync, what else would you call it? Just remember that all parties come to an end. The participants have their attention on the emotions they're experiencing. But notice: They are surrounded by plant life, the inevitable presence of the material world.

4 OF CUPS: The querent has three cups before him. They are either empty or not to his liking. This has left him in a

disgruntled state. But he is being offered another cup that could satisfy him! He is either blind to it or refuses to give it his attention. Are you so focused on your losses that you ignore new possibilities for happiness?

5 OF CUPS: Here, the querent is even deeper within his regrets about the past. There are always new possibilities for expansion, but you must face them and be willing to move beyond the past. Also, notice that a river lies just beyond the querent. You may have lost the emotions you've known in the past, but there are always new joys to sustain you. They will take different forms and may not

Be as exciting or have the same flavor as before, but they will sustain you. The old forms are always changing. Clinging only brings despair.

6 OF CUPS: The emotions of this card are simple, nostalgic, or childish. They are based on a child's view of the material world (symbolized by cups full of flowers), uncomplicated by the larger burdens of life. Both the boy and the girl have their vision blocked by this view of the world. Yet, like all aspects of our awareness, it is invented. It may be enjoyed for what it is.

7 OF CUPS: This is a card of possibilities, of forking paths. Each will lead you to a slightly different emotion. When this card comes up, ask yourself: Which cup is my attention being drawn to? Also, do not assume that any of the cups are bad or good. You do not know who lies beneath the covered figure. You do not know if the snake or dragon are allies or enemies.

This card will teach you that you assign meaning to situations. Also, notice that the querent's form is shadowy. Without a person to reflect on them, these objects can carry no emotion.

8 OF CUPS: This card always makes me think of a retreat from emotion. The cups have been left behind. The traveler has crossed a stream and is hiking into the realm of sensory materialism. The dreamy qualities of the moon may still be overhead, the water may be nearby, but the querent is trying to stay on firm ground. There are many times when it pays to turn your emotions down. Similarly, there are times when emotions are required. Consider which is best for the current situation.

9 OF CUPS: I like to call this card the merchant of feelings. Like a store owner, he has access to a (nearly) full range of emotional experiences. But they sit behind him. He is not using them. He can access them at any time, but he is glad just to help others find the emotions they seek (and profit from the transaction). He is firmly grounded and content, and in a very powerful position.

10 OF CUPS: Unlike card 9, card 10 is fully experiencing the spectrum of emotions. It is exhilarating and joyous. It may be likened to a supernatural experience. Like rainbows, understanding the science behind your emotions does not lessen their effect.

THE PAGE OF CUPS: The page is the simplest stirring of emotion. It will make the querent curious for more and is hardly satisfying.

THE KNIGHT OF CUPS: The feeling behind the knight is noticeably stronger than the page. For me, the knight cards are usually the point when a call to action takes over. A person feeling this emotion cannot suppress it (as can be done with the page). This card may be compared to overwhelming hunger for an emotion. If that desire can be fulfilled, excellent. If not, the knight will experience frustration.

THE QUEEN OF CUPS: The queen's emotional state is nearly overwhelming. The water is nearly at her toes. But she is still on land. Nevertheless, this level of emotional involvement is either blissful or hellish, depending on the circumstances.

THE KING OF CUPS: The king represents the purest feeling of a complete emotional experience. There is no logic, creativity, or sensory awareness. There is only pure emotion. He is completely afloat on turbulent waters. If he is a strong king, he will survive and eventually reach land. If he is weak and the water grows too rough, the emotion may drown him.

PENTACLES (DISKS)

The material world, which we know through our senses, is the realm of the Pentacles. It is the most grounded of suits, and thus associated with the element earth. If you want to deal with the practical, the pragmatic, and the sensible, then Pentacles are for you. All that you find in the world before you mask it with your thoughts and feelings is the domain of pentacles. This suit also deals with responsibility – think of boy scouts and girl scouts and their emphasis on survival skills.

Here are some examples of Pentacles:

Rain falls on a sidewalk.
You sweep the dust off your floor.
Two cars collide.
The power goes off in your house.
A volcano erupts.
You itch your leg.
Dominos fall.
Your freezer turns water into ice.
A factory assembles a ship.
You lift weights at the gym.
Cats are meowing in an alley.
A flower blossoms.

Here are my interpretations of the Pentacles cards:

ACE OF PENTACLES – The Ace cards are typically the pure manifestation of the element. With Pentacles, this looks like the Garden of Eden. Human consciousness has not yet intruded upon the earthly realm, and nature is in a pure state.

2 PENTACLES – A person with his hands full, overwhelmed by life. Not only are his hands tied by his world, but his emotions (the water behind him) are messy. This is not a person enjoying life, but a person constrained by it.

3 OF PENTACLES – This card is about collaboration to make something in the physical world. The planner and the priest oversee the worker. All three people have different visions for what they are creating, but compromises are necessary for collaboration.

4 OF PENTACLES – At this stage, the man has a firm grip on his material reality. His world has been managed and controlled. This control may be satisfying, or it may lead to his undoing.

5 OF PENTACLES – This is a stage of physical suffering. Perhaps you lost your job, or your house has been repossessed, or you broke your leg. The loss is material, in some sense. Notice that these two people are outside the church, signifying their spiritual emptiness. The loss may be physical, but they always have access to the spiritual realm.

6 OF PENTACLES – This is a stage of prosperity, and giving back to others. But as you do so, you remember how much you have. You're careful not to give **too** much away. You may be **lending** and keeping a strict account of all you give. This could be a prosperous businessman, or affluent parents providing for a child.

7 OF PENTACLES – Much work has been done, and this has led to a material harvest. It may be savings for retirement or other stockpiling of wealth. It may be a house acquired after years of hard work or some other form of security.

8 OF PENTACLES – This card is a position of order and connection to the world. The man knows his role and fills it. He is satisfied with his work and has no time for frivolous activity.

9 OF PENTACLES – This card is a position of comfort and satisfaction, a period of great success with life. This person may, however, be disconnected from the community at large.

As often is the case, when we are happy, we forget those who are miserable.

10 OF PENTACLES – This person is extremely comfortable in the world. Perhaps he has even retired from the hustle and bustle of the world at large. Others may view him as obsolete or in decline. His comfort is assured, but he may be dissatisfied with his existence like there is still something lacking, or more to live.

PAGE OF PENTACLES – The Page of Pentacles is like a child in nature. It could be a person leaving school or the office after many years. It is a confrontation with the physical stuff of existence.

KNIGHT OF PENTACLES – The knight is much more comfortable with the concrete nature of life. This could be a national park ranger or just someone who can look beyond the signs and symbols of culture and experience what is actually present in the world.

QUEEN OF PENTACLES – The passive aspects of the physical world. The queen is all that is reserved and quiet in the world. She is a gentle breeze, the peace, and the quiet of nature. Things are always happening at some level, but through the queen, they are most relaxed.

KING OF PENTACLES – The king is in full control of his world. He completely understands how the physical processes of life and nature function. He may also signify great wealth, comfort, and abundance. He does not get caught up in the turbulence of emotions.

WANDS

Wands are the suit of creativity, intuition, and spontaneity. A magician's wand is a channel for energy, and your imagination does the same thing. Organizing this energy is the work of swords and pentacles, but the energy itself flows through the wand. Its element is fire, which radiates heat. But fire can also get out of control and destroy.

Here are some examples of Wands at work:

You paint a picture of the first thing that comes to your mind.
You make up a song on the piano.
A story idea comes to you from out of the blue.
A vision of your dream house appears effortlessly in your mind.
You are interviewing candidates for a job, and you pick one intuitively, not logically.
You have vivid dreams while sleeping.
You imagine the best way to decorate your home.
You write a bucket list of the fun things you want to do.
You imagine a new possibility for software that has never been done before.
You come up with different uses for a space in your community.

Here are my interpretations of the Wands:

ACE OF WANDS – The ace is the eruption of a suit into the querent's life. Which is not to say that the element was absent beforehand, only that the element is making its presence felt in a larger way. With wands, this is the opening of the imagination, the realm of the possible. Imagination is a playful place full of possibility, and it is best approached with a child's attitude of adventure.

2 OF WANDS – This is early in the stage of imaginative or spiritual exploration. The man is secure in his castle, but he sees the potential in the world all around him. This is a card of infinite possibilities that recalls the phrase, Who dares, wins.

3 OF WANDS – This is a more challenging position for the querent. A desert surrounds him. On the other hand, the man uses his wands as strong support. His inner strength may make up for a lack in the outer world.

4 OF WANDS – Humanity is seen from a distance. A celebration, party, or drunken feast is taking place, but the querent is distant. How does humanity appear to you here? Do you see them as good? Or do you despise them and want to keep your distance? Whatever the case, you are adding to the scene's texture. Notice how wands, connected with spiritual energy, are united with plant life (pentacles, or material energy).

5 OF WANDS – In this card, we see a clash of worldviews. The boy who holds his wand the highest is the one most removed from the battle. If you enjoy argumentation, you may want to stay in the battle – otherwise, it may be beneficial to step away. True creativity does not worry about rewards or esteem from the world. It is only interested in the act of creation.

6 OF WANDS – This is a card of victory and smooth sailing (perhaps after the contention of the previous card). The horse's rider may be smug and satisfied, but he is hardly in a position to create.

7 OF WANDS – This is a card of energetic creation. Unlike card 5, the querent is in a better position to operate in the world. Here, his creativity is based on responding to the work of others. Much like dancing, this kind of creation is impossible alone.

8 OF WANDS –Something is about to be determined, as these wands are up in the air. All four elements are in this card. Air is already acting upon the energy of the wands, trying to organize it. Earth and water wait to see how the wands shall land. A creative endeavor may be underway, and for

Now, it cannot be stopped.

9 OF WANDS – The act of creation has been accomplished, but this is not a creative card. The work is done; the man looks at his accomplishments. If he rests on his laurels and becomes transfixed by his past work, he will be unable to create anew. He must break new ground or else the wands will act as a cage.

10 OF WANDS – Here the querent is trying to move forward creatively. He still clings to his past. He sees his future through his previous endeavors. He is unwilling to let go. For creativity to be free, it cannot be held to yesterday's rules. On the other hand, the querent may be taking his ideas to sell to a company, for example. That may be appropriate now – just

recognize that it will not be a **creative** act, and it is better handled by the intellect of swords.

THE PAGE OF WANDS – This is the young artist or spiritual novice attempting a new creation. The work may be unimpressive at this point, but **he** is impressed with himself. Did this really come from him? Many people dabble with creation at this level and take it no further.

THE KNIGHT OF WANDS – The knight has honed his craft and is about to release his energy into the act of creation. This card can also indicate someone making deeper inroads into a spiritual practice.

THE QUEEN OF WANDS – The queen is the passive recipient of the imagination's rewards. At this point, creativity is automatic. The artist can engage with his or her art, and a unique outcome is guaranteed. The black cat and the bright sunflower seem to indicate a person who can channel the positive and negative forces of creation.

THE KING WANDS – The king is the master of the element of fire. It burns within him at full force, but he can control it. He can conceive anything, and creativity is second nature to him. To **not** create would be difficult at this point. Among the kings, he has the most potential to create and destroy – only the King of Swords, through a rational organization, can possibly overcome him.

Chapter Four

How to Use Your Tarot Cards

<u>Conversing with The Tarot</u>

With a general understanding of the Major and Minor Arcana, you will be ready to work with the tarot. More than anything, it can offer you advice and help you view situations more clearly.

One way to consult the tarot is to use a **spread**. A spread is simply a way to lay out cards in specific positions. Based on a card's position in a spread, it will have a particular meaning. There are many, many spreads. Personally, I think there is an overemphasis on spreads in the tarot literature. It may be helpful to know what a card in a certain place means, but you can get the same information by simply asking better questions of the tarot. Because spreads can confuse beginners, I'm not going to use them in this book.

It is more important when getting started to grow comfortable with the cards themselves. Learn to assess your feelings about them. If this feels too free-form for you, remember that somebody **invented** every spread in use. Just as every religious orthodoxy and ceremony was once new, spreads are an arbitrary creation. You may adopt the traditions of others – this can be powerful – but it can be more liberating to create your own traditions. How you approach tarot reflects how you approach life. If you find you need a spread, they are easily found online and in books.

To begin getting advice from the cards, start with simple questions. When you put a question to the tarot, you are essentially questioning yourself and the larger Self that includes all of the universe. You can ask simple information questions (yes or no questions, for example), but better questions will yield better answers. So while you can ask questions like, Should, I buy this house? – the phrasing of that question raises a lot of problems. Should you buy this house according to **whom**? Should you buy it if you really want a secure place to live? Should you buy it if you want more freedom? The question supposes that you are a creature incapable of independent thought and need to be told what you **should** do.

But let's say you still want **advice** about buying a certain house. With that in mind, you can ask the question differently:

What outcome can I expect by buying this house?

Or

How happy will I be living in this house?

These types of questions go beyond a binary of yes and no. Every situation has its positive and negative aspects. By asking open-ended questions, you allow for more nuance in your tarot's answers.

Picking a card is once again, completely up to you. My method: shuffle the cards, clear my mind, and relax. I'll often close my eyes and ask my question to myself. Approach the tarot as you approach your highest self: with patience, gratitude, and reverence. I will often cut the deck and take the card I find. Sometimes I spread all of the cards out and slowly hover my hand over them. When it feels right, I take the card my finger is over.

If this all seems arbitrary and random, it may well be. But in choosing a card, the tarot seems to give you the card you need. The answer may seem wrong or even like a joke. It may seem like the exact opposite of an appropriate answer. When this happens, the tarot may be shining a spotlight on some aspect of a situation you're neglecting. Instead of giving you an answer you want, the tarot can steer you toward a necessary confrontation. Also, consider the frame of mind that needs a specific answer. **How** you converse with the tarot will teach you more than any specific answer.

As you shuffle your deck, sometimes a card will spontaneously fall out. I call this kind of card a jumper. Rather than put it back in the deck, I allow that this card so eagerly wanted to reveal itself that it jumped to my attention. Is it silly to anthropomorphize an inert card? Sure, but no more than

Using the tarot itself. If you accidentally come across an old friend while walking down the street, you give it meaning. It stirs up memories in the brain and steers you down a different road. You may have a completely different day because of that chance meeting. The cards you select in the tarot have the same activating principle. If you leave home ten minutes later than usual, you will have a completely different day. It may be similar in the grand scheme of things, but it will be different in details. And sometimes these details add up and send you into a totally different universe.

Once a card is chosen, take some time to study it. What kind of energy does it emote? Any work of art has energy. An action movie might get you excited. A gentle piece of classical music can help you get to sleep. It is virtually impossible to create a work of art without some kind of energy. Energy is its own brand of information. So consider the feeling you get from the card.

Also, consider what associations it brings. Journaling about a card can help you look deeper into what it's trying to tell you. Wherever your mind goes is where it needs to go. All the tarot does is stir up the necessary contents that are already inside you.

If, for example, I have some free time on Sunday, I might ask, What is the best way to spend Sunday? If the card that comes up is the Ace of Wands, it seems that some sort of creative or spiritual activity might be a good choice. I've been involved with writing and meditation groups, and I remember that I haven't done either in a while. That might be the best use of my time for Sunday. Obviously, the tarot isn't **telling** me what to do. But it shines a spotlight on my mind's contents.

Another example: I ask the tarot, Would now be a good time to get a dog? The card I pull from the deck is the 18th card of the Major Arcana, the Moon. The Moon card actually has a dog on it! But I look at that dog howling at the moon with the wolf, and I remember the wild energy a dog has. As fun as it would be to have a dog, it would be a lot of responsibility, and it would probably be better to wait a while longer. At least until I have more time and room for a dog. Once again, the tarot has not **told** me whether I should get a dog. It has only helped me see the situation more clearly.

In this way, the tarot can help you find a solution to any dilemma. In addition to journaling, here are some other ways to work with the tarot.

DO A DAILY READING

You can consult the tarot without having a specific question. In the morning, simply ask the tarot for a card appropriate for that day. I'll often ask for three cards. It's surprising how all three cards will work their way into my day.

USE A CARD AS YOUR PHONE OR DESKTOP BACKGROUND

I often ask the tarot for a necessary phone background for the month. This may be a lesson or mindset I will be working on. Having it on my phone guarantees, I will think about it throughout the month. Putting it on your computer as your desktop background also works.

MEDITATE ON AN IMAGE

You can sit comfortably, relax your mind, and take an image in. Turning off rational thought may be the best way to approach this exercise. It will allow you to connect to the card's energy and enter that state of being. You can do this with your eyes open and look at the card itself, or with your eyes closed, holding the image in your mind.

MAKE ART FROM THE CARDS

A card can inspire a work of art. You might do a painting or sculpture based on a card. It doesn't have to look anything like the original. It is ultimately about your mind, not the card. Similarly, you could write a story, poem, song, or something else based on the card. What scenario does the card suggest to you? If you are an actor, try to become the character on the card. Follow your intuition.

When you return to the card, you may find that its meaning has opened up for you.

START OR JOIN A TAROT GROUP

A tarot group lets you tap into the collective wisdom of others, and see things that would otherwise be impossible. Also, you'll be able to help others see through their tarot blind spots.

FIND TAROT CORRESPONDENCES

Can you connect the tarot to other things? Sure. Whether it's the Teenage Mutant Ninja Turtles, the Myers-Briggs personality types, the Beatles, or Harry Potter houses, there is no shortage of correspondences that can be made with the tarot. Doing this will allow you to see the larger patterns that the tarot indicates.

STUDY TAROT LITERATURE

Every book or video about the tarot can add to your collective knowledge. In addition to standard texts, fiction such as **Gravity's Rainbow, Illuminatus!** And the comic book

Promethea were helpful for getting my head around the cards.

MAKE YOUR OWN TAROT DECK

The tarot should be as personal as possible. At the very least, make a conscious choice about the deck you use, finding one that resonates with you. But if you feel up to the challenge, make your own deck. This can be done with colored pencil on 3 x 5 cards, as paintings, digitally, or however, you choose.

Chapter Five
Card Combinations, Patterns and Elemental Dignities

As a proficient reader when you have two cards that come up in a reading that has a similar meaning, it's really quite subtle, so it's important to make sure that your customers or subjects really understand the message that's been given to them. There are several ways that you can end up finding patterns in reading. In this section, we'll focus on the most common examples of cards that often come up in a reading or the cards that are often paired so that you can see the patterns of how to read these card combinations and hopefully derived a much stronger message out of them that could be relevant to your subject.

Similar Meanings

The similarity of meanings and card combinations can be adjusted or change depending on which card it is paired with. Examples of cards that often come up and have a relatively similar meaning are the Seven of Pentacles and the Knight of Pentacles; the Eight of Swords and the Devil Card; Two of Cups and Five of Cups; Ten of Swords and Wheel of Fortune. Take note though that these cards can come with other pairs or come up more often, it can come in various ways, but it's almost as if these cards are carrying around the same energy with them.

The Seven of Pentacles and the Knight of Pentacles

The Seven of Pentacles have meaning associated with attention to detail, diligence, patience; sometimes it signifies delayed results or slow progress that could be happening in your subject's life. It can also mean that the person has not been really able to harvest or get results on whatever he/she is working on, so it generally means that the person could be working hard, putting a lot of effort and being patient in order to reap the rewards. Often times, this card is paired with Knight of Pentacles which has some sort of similar connotations, (of course if the Seven of Pentacles is paired with a different card, it will have a totally different meaning), the Knight of Pentacles or sometimes referred to as the Prince of Pentacles can often relate to stability, loyalty, being very practical, pragmatic and a card that associates with seeking security, does things slowly, someone who thinks about the kind of effort that he/she is willing to put into in order to achieve a certain growth or progress without rushing in.

So from all these meanings and associated adjectives, you can see that from the two cards, there are similarities of meanings – there's slowness, practicality, pragmatism, there's also steady of progress, and the theme of "not reaping the rewards immediately unless much effort is exerted." These will be the highlights when the two cards come up, so from those similar meanings, you can easily interpret that your subject might not be reaching fulfillment, completion or success at this point of their lives and that they may need to be patient because there will be a steady but slow progress that will be happening.

These meanings that you draw from the similar connotations of both cards can be related to your subject's career, relationship, dreams etc. Which means that they might need to be patient in their work or perhaps put in a lot of effort in their relationships; it could be reliable but steady not necessarily full of passion but perhaps practicality.

Now if the Seven of Pentacles is paired with a different card, say, for example, the Hanged Man, it can have a sort of similar meaning, but the focus of the message will most likely be different. The Hanged Man card is associated with words like surrender, pause, reflection, inaction, and standstill. It is still related to the meaning of the Seven of Pentacles because the theme is all about something that is not coming to fruition right away, but in this case, it could be less on the practicality or hard work. Perhaps, the focus of the message is that the rewards will definitely be delayed due to some kind of standstill along the way.

These meanings were derived simply because that's the strongest common denominator between the two cards, so as a tarot card reader that's what you should highlight more. These are some examples where parts of them have a similar meaning, which is why the message becomes very strong in the reading.

The Eight of Swords and the Devil Card

These cards again have similar meanings; the Eight of Swords is a card that is associated with self – limitation, it often means that the subject could be restricting themselves and not moving out of the situation even if he/she can. This card also means that there's a lack of clarity and vision or sort of self – entrapment because the subject may not know where he/she is going and have no idea how to get there.

The Devil Card, on the other hand, is associated with meanings like temptation, attachment to things, and entrapment, but it's more about dealing with one's 'inner demons' or inner imprisonment. It could also mean attaching oneself to something that is not healthy or good. So from the meaning of these two cards, you can focus on the part that they are binding themselves to a thought or belief system as well as to things or people that could be limiting your subject and not allowing them to be free. There's an attachment issue, self – entrapment or self – limitation.

Now, if you paired the Devil Card with the Seven of Cups, it can again have a similar meaning, but the focus of the message is different. As with the Seven of Cups, it's a card associated with imagination, visions, delusions, skewed perspective, and moving to things that are not in your best interest. Most of the time, this card represents substance abuse if the person is in a difficult situation, so if this card is paired with the Devil Card (with a meaning of attachment to things that aren't healthy), the message you can focus on is that your subject could be attaching or depending themselves on something like a substance, toxic relationships or something that is not healthy.

Two of Cups and Five of Cups

The Two of Cups is about making a connection with others and building a bond with people. The Five of Cups, on the other hand, is also about a person's emotional life, intuition, feelings and relationships with others, how a person reconciles things, and about the inner world. So if you encounter pulling out two or more cups in a reading, that means that your subject is dealing with some kind of emotional part of themselves or relationship situations. In this case, you can interpret it as something that's been a loss (probably due to a breakup or death of a loved one) and your subject may need to be positive about it. So if it's a relationship issue, it means that your subject should look at the positive side of it even if it could be something of a breakup, you could advise him/her to let go or move on.

If the Two of Cups is paired with a Three of Cups, there's still a cup theme (or a relationship theme), but it's with more than one person like friendships, family, etc. It represents your communication with others or positive connection with people. So if these two cards are paired, you can interpret it in a way where there's the emotional situation going on but it's on a positive level, and it's more than one person. The point is you're looking for a pattern, but each cup has a different meaning or has your subject is focusing on a different area at the moment.

Ten of Swords and Wheel of Fortune

The number ten usually means that you're nearing the end of the cycle or you're at the end of the cycle, so that could mean that the person has gone through a lot or have experienced a lot of things already. The number ten is the closing of a cycle; the swords represent some challenges that a person has been through. So the Ten of Swords card has come to a point where a person is in a collapse kind of situation. However, it's also saying that a new cycle is about to begin, so the person has to take a look at how you can prepare for that next cycle.

The Ten of Swords is connected to the Wheel of Fortune because the Wheel of Fortune card represents a cyclical nature of things, so that means that a person goes through phases and move from one to another, there's always a change or flux, and it also talks about the "seasons of life." These card combinations can mean that your subject is at the end of that particular situation or even in their life – that they're probably about to close that "chapter" but a new one is coming.

Elemental Dignities

Essentially elemental dignities will make you determine if the card is well – dignified or ill – dignified. It also depends on what another card combination is next to it. You'll learn if a card combination has an element that speaks the same language or the opposite language. Elemental dignities basically pertain to the relationships of each element to one another.

Qualities of Elements

Before determining the relationship of each element, you must first know the qualities or characteristics of the elements in a card. Just like in any other field, particularly subjects that deal with nature or energy fields, the elements are composed of Air, Fire, Water, and Earth. In Tarot cards, the air element is represented by swords, the water element is represented by cups, the Earth element is pentacles, and the fire is represented by wands. The four elements relate to the four kinds found in the tarot deck. By looking at the four elements, a reader can determine some of its characteristics.

There's also the concept of polarity in the four elements which is also divided by two; the first pair is Fire (Wands) and Air (Swords) which are also called active elements; the second pair is Water (Cups) and Earth (Pentacles) which are also called passive elements. The former paired elements are masculine, and the latter pair is feminine.

Masculine elements are active, outgoing, extroverted, and have a "yang energy." It can also be described as direct, assertive, sustaining, autonomous, and often times self – motivated. These masculine elements also focus on the self, and its 'powers' come from within oneself. On the other hand, the feminine elements have characteristics that are receptive, indirect, passive, introverted, soft, intuitive, nurturing and it has a tendency to look outside of oneself especially for advice or verifications.

Elemental Dignities and its Relationships

Now that you've learned what the elements are and their representation in the tarot deck, the next important thing to know is how these elements relate to one another. As a reader, you're going to encounter combinations that come up in readings so you have to know its meaning and relationships because it can also affect the message of the cards.

The fire element is usually opposite the water, which makes sense because water can put out a fire, so having these elements means that they weaken one another. Once these elements show up in a reading, you can easily determine that those opposing energies are weakening one another and there's also a flux between these two characteristics or aspects of life that are showing up. Another elemental pairs that weaken each other is air and earth because the air is above and the earth is below.

Cards of the same element like fire (wands) and air (swords) which are also masculine strengthen each other. On the other hand, feminine elements like water (cups) and earth (pentacles) also speak the same language, which therefore strengthens each other as well. Elements that neutralized each other are fire to earth as well as air to water. These things could be quite hard to remember, but what you can do is to give them acronyms or have your own method of memorizing these concepts so you can easily relate it during your readings.

So basically when a card is 'elementally well dignified' that means it is being strengthened by the card next to it, on the other hand, if a card is 'elementally ill dignified' it is being weakened by the card beside it. So if for example, a card shows up and it's a sword, and then it is next to another sword then it is at its strongest point because it can express its full potential and therefore elementally well dignified. If a card is in the same suit, it's going to speak the same language and vice – versa. So if you pulled a sword (air) and the card next to it is a pentacle (earth), it weakens one another, and therefore it is elementally ill dignified.

Well – Dignified (Strong Position) Cards

In this section, you'll learn some examples of what it means to have a well – dignified cards. These cards have similar polarity (either masculine or feminine) elemental energy to it. We'll take a look at the Three of Wands and King of Wands; Three of Wands and King of Swords for the well – dignified cards and the Eight of Pentacles and Knight of Swords for the ill – dignified examples.

Three of Wands and King of Wands

As what you've learned, wand cards are equal to the fire element and therefore has a masculine energy that is well dignified. These cards have similar characteristics; it is active, outgoing, and has clarity in the decision – making the process. So once these two cards are pulled, it can mean that your subject has a significant amount of masculine energy and that he/she is not going to have difficulty in terms of focus or being direct. They will pretty much force themselves to make something happen to accomplish a particular goal; they could also be assertive and self – motivated. So studying the elemental aspect of the cards can make a reader say not just the meaning of the cards or literal interpretation of it but also be able to recognize the polarity of the elements it represents.

As you can see the card is well dignified and therefore is at its highest expression if you look at it this way.

Three of Wands and King of Swords

As what you've learned earlier wands are represented by fire and swords are represented by air, which is another masculine energy. It may not be quite well – dignified compared to Three of Wands card and the King of Wands card (since it's basically of the same element) but it's still well positioned because they're speaking the same language – the more outgoing masculine language and because fire strengthens air and vice – versa. So if the King of Swords is paired with the Three of Wands your subject may have created something to a certain point but at this point must make certain logical decisions or really analyze something to create a sound decision going forward.

Four of Cups and Four of Pentacles

Cups (water) and Pentacles (earth) are both feminine polarity. They share characteristics that are receptive, passive, introverted, and have a tendency to look on the outside to figure out what to do. Since they are both feminine, they are well-dignified cards and the fact that their numbers are the same means that they also speak the same language, so it has a lot of similarities to it however, this is where you have too much passive energy and potentially too little progress wherein a person could feel as if they're being controlled by other things or being in a passive position.

The number four signifies stability, but it can also mean that there could be intrinsic limitations that prevent an individual from growing or achieving something. If you pulled out a bunch of feminine energy and the number four, then there's a lot of passivity or stagnation or maybe that individual is stuck in a certain position and that the only way is to take a risk to be able to get out of that restriction to be able to learn. You can also advise your subject to get in touch with more masculine energy in order to help them to move forward or get out of their own "box." On the other hand, if you pulled out cards and saw a lot of active masculine energy it could mean that there's conflict, fight or competition, the solution is to get in touch with the female elements or passive principles.

Ill – Dignified (Weak Position) Card

The examples in this section will focus on cards that are opposite each other or weakened by the card next to it.

Eight of Pentacles and Knight of Swords

The Eight of Pentacles is an earth element, and the Knight of Swords is an air element which means they are opposite and therefore weakening each other and not speaking the same language. The Knight of Swords card has a masculine polarity to it since it is an air element; it has characteristics of being action-oriented, outgoing, adventurous, flexible, and pretty much has masculine energy to it. Pentacles, in general, are all about manifestations in the physical realm, it has tendencies to move slower and only working on things that are tangible and kind of earthbound. When it comes to the Eight of Pentacles represent someone who diligently works, takes time to develop a skill and someone who is working very hard over a long period of time.

So if you think about it, the Eight of Pentacles is all about taking one's time to create something while the Knight of Swords focuses on direct action and just going after whatever idea comes to mind. These characteristics are opposing and doesn't go very well together, if your subject pulled this card combination, it could mean that they are in a flux between these two opposing energies so most likely these energies are fighting against one another or perhaps your subject needs to be aware it because it's not going to help them in moving forward.

Your subject may also need some sort of compromise to these two opposing elements in order to bring things in harmony or balance. It could also mean that the Eight of Pentacles need to accept the brilliant ideas of the Knight of Swords, and the Knight of Swords should need to slow down and take time to think things out. So you need to let your subject know that they have opposing energies that they need to be aware of and work out.

Chapter Six
Card Placements within a Tarot Spread

In this section, you'll learn some of the ways in which a card is strengthened or weakened depending on the placement within a reading; it can be related to an elemental dignity or other meanings. Knowing the card placement or even card reversal within a tarot spread can affect your reading as well. I'm going to give you some examples of how card placement may have an impact on the meaning of the card and how it is strengthened or weakened by being in a particular position.

Cards That Fall in an Outcome/Final/Future Position

Many different spreads have some type of outcome or final position, so if you have that kind of spread for your subject, you'll know that those cards are in a very strong position because it's showing you a final outcome or a point of completion.

- **Six of Wands** - Six of Wands, six is a number that represents a certain level of completion; it's also a card that celebrates victory in a positive way.
- **Ten of Pentacles** - Ten of Pentacles is another great card in the outcome position, if you have a ten that shows up even in other types of cards, it usually signifies a final point in some type of cycle, as for Ten of Pentacles, it's a positive outcome for some kind of success in career, relationships, family or

other areas. If the ten is in the Swords card or Wands, it could be quite a challenging end or one that has been through strife compared to cups and pentacles. But again, seeing a ten is great because it means that the cycle is in a final point and a new cycle is coming.

- **The World -** The World card in itself is already showing an outcome or completion as well; it also means putting an effort over a period of time and seeing success on a physical level. It can also have a spiritual connotation, and it's a well-dignified card because it's in a very strong position.

- **The Sun** - The Sun card in a final position means a positive outlook; it also shows confidence and just a naturally strong card to have for the outcome.

- **The Ten of Cups** - Ten of Cups shows happiness, connections with loved ones, abundance, and a lot of great things have happened for an individual. It also signifies an emotional satisfaction.

- **The Wheel of Fortune -** The Wheel of Fortune again shows a level of completion in phases or cycles. You can assume that one cycle is ending and another one will begin soon. This card also holds a strong position in the outcome reading.

Cards that Fall in a Challenge or Obstacle Position

Cards that are in positive positions aren't the only cards that are strengthened because what we're talking about here in this chapter is whether a card is well dignified in the sense of its meaning. The card must be in its purest meaning when it comes up, so cards that are challenging or difficult in reading must be something that your client or subject might need to overcome.

- **Three of Swords** – is a card that shows separation, difficulty, and denotes some kind of pain or anger that has been caused by difficult relationships that can be felt at a very deep level. So if this card comes up in a challenge position, it's about how your subject can overcome the pain and difficulty that he/she has experienced and how to deal with it.
- **The Devil Card** – the devil card denotes some form of attachment mentally or physically that might be holding your subject back from being whoever he/she wants to be or do.
- **Five of Cups** – this card denotes that one should overcome some sort of grief or despair that he/she sometimes feel and go through. Your subject should learn how to deal with those emotions as best as they can to move forward.
- **Nine of Swords** - this card in a challenge position denotes that one should overcome personal anxieties or difficulties. Your subject should believe in his/herself and not over - analyzed everything mentally.

Reading Cards in Tarot Spread Position

In this section, you'll learn how to read a negative card in a positive placement or vice – versa. Tarot cards, in general looks at the scope of a human's life or an individual's psyche and how we live our lives. Every card in the tarot conveys some kind of lesson that you can learn from whether it's in a positive or negative position. You need to understand that nothing is black and white – which means that nothing is completely positive or negative; there are always two sides to it and a lesson to learn from.

Positive Cards in a Negative Placement vs. Negative Cards in a Positive Placement

This concept can be very hard to grasp especially if you're a beginner it's because most newbie readers read cards in its literal form or the meaning of it, but if the card is placed in a contradicting situation, it can be hard to analyze and draw meaning from. As with most expert tarot card readers, they have developed their own reading system in reading cards that are either in a negative or positive placement but their common denominator or perhaps the guiding principle is that tarot cards are not one dimensional, even if it's a positive cards there'll still be some negative aspect to it, same with negative cards. Some readers refer to it as a shadow, warning, or edge if a card has positive meaning but is placed in a negative position or vice – versa. If you understand the edge or shadows of a card, you'll be able to understand how to read them in any kind of placement. Here are some examples:

- **The Sun Card**

The Sun card is a positive card, so if it lands in an outcome or final position within a spread, then you can automatically say that it will be about optimism, happiness, fulfillment or a person has shone in its own way in life because that's the usual denotation of that card. Now, if the Sun Card comes up in a negative position, it may denote that your subject may not be living life to the fullest, they may not be acknowledging the joys in their life, your client may not be fully expressing who they are or who they want to be or what if your client does not feel free to express something or may not have the freedom to live life on their own terms. Those are the ideas that you could ask or share to your client if a positive card like this comes up in a negative position.

- **Three of Swords**

The Three of Swords card is a difficult card or a negative card because it usually denotes pain, separation, betrayal, isolation, heartbreak, and suffering. So if this card comes up in a positive placement, the edge or shadow of this card could be a call for healing. The lesson or the message you can convey to your client is to determine how one can start the healing process or identify and acknowledge those sufferings so that they'll be able to start healing in that particular area of their life. If your client is asking for advice and this card comes up, then you can tell him/her to face the pain they are feeling and possibly do something with what could help them heal a particular feeling or angst they may have.

- **The Emperor Card**

The Emperor card is all about structure, order, formation so it can be related to rules and regulations. It also has some kind of authority or leadership quality to it. It's a positive card that could be great if pulled in an outcome position because it can mean that one is becoming a leader or perhaps one needs to pay attention to a structure to maintain an orderly kind of environment. But if this card is in a negative position, it can mean that the power or control brought about by leadership can be too much to handle. It can mean that an individual is overpowering or over - controlling a situation; there are probably too many rules, laws or regulations that can be a hindrance to freedom or creativity; it can also mean that a person is too limited in his/her approach and he/she may need to let go of some of these limiting beliefs. So if this card is in a negative placement, it will focus on how much control or power is happening as well as how the structure may limit freedom to a person or to other people.

- **Nine of Swords**

The Nine of Swords is a negative card that's all about anxiety, mental anguish, depression and some sort of feedback loop where a person is constantly thinking about something that's painful or obsessing about something that is bothering him/her for a long time. It could also bring up a level of being ill due to a stressful situation. There's a lot of strife and isolation for this card but if the Nine of Swords comes up in a positive position, the advice you can give to your subject to overcome a situation is to maybe be able to step back and figure out what it is that's causing them these anxieties so they can find a way to solve it, kind of getting to the root cause of the problem. Another meaning you can derive from this card in a positive way is again healing, so perhaps this card is telling your subject to take time to heal and just let it all out, let all the tears flow so that he/she can be cleanse inside out and be able to let go of all the things that is troubling them and move past this difficulty.

- **Nine of Cups**

The Nine of Cups denotes that one hasn't reached the end yet, but they're almost there. It's a positive card that represents one's emotional self or inner world, relationship with oneself or with others, creativity and the likes (remember it's a feminine polarity). It also means that a person has reached a certain level of abundance or fulfillment, but they are alone. So the edge of this card, if it's placed in a negative position, is that the person is "alone," meaning that the individual may not be connecting or sharing what they have accomplished with other people. You can also consider a level of complacency as well as overindulgence in the individual's part.

- **The Five of Cups**

The Five of Cups has an intrinsic edge to it; as you now know, the cups talks all about relationships, emotions, inner world, creativity, and intuition. This card, in particular, denotes loss, grief, emotional pain, and difficult to let go so this is in itself a negative card. So the edge of the card, when it is placed in a positive position, is that there's some kind of hope after all this pain and strife, and it means that an individual needs to let go of whatever he/she lose in order to move on to see the positive things that are still there.

Three Card Spreads

Three card spreads are usually used to see what's coming up for the next three months or possibly the kind of events that will unfold with regards to the subject's physical, mental or even emotional aspect. What you can do is to let your client choose one card for each of the next three months for them to have a glimpse of the future. If you're doing to a three card spread what you can do is to assign the first card that is picked for the next month (not the month you are in), and then the next card is for the consecutive month and so on. In this section, we'll give you some examples of how to read cards that could mean the next three months for your subject.

Example #1: The Four of Cups, Ace of Wands, Four of Wands

This is where the other lessons will come in, so if you remember the principle of elemental dignities you can use that in initially reading the cards and incorporate other tarot reading principles from there.

From this set of example, you'll notice that Wands card are predominant since there are two out of three. The predominance of wands or the fire element energy is going to be important for the next three months. It could mean that an individual may develop some type of interest or passion in some endeavor or a certain drive and energy. They might also use a more masculine polarity, which means that they'll probably be more action-oriented in order to achieve something. They'll also probably start off the next three months with the cup energy, which means that there could be an emotional element involved.

You can also take a look at another aspect, which is the numbers of the cards. So from this example, there are a four of cups and four of wands the number four signifies structure, order, stability, limitation, and there's possibly a manifestation in the physical world. So you can look at it in the way of the flow of events, will there be a stagnation in the next three months or what kind of progress is going to happen, is it from stagnation to action or vice – versa, etc. So from this example, the four of cups (the first month) denotes stagnation, the ace of wands denotes not much action; the four of wands denotes a significant form of action, so that could be the possible flow in the next three months.

The advice you can give to your client is that in the first month (four of cups) they may want to determine what's stopping them from doing something or focus on the possible opportunities around them. You can also suggest feeling their emotions about certain things but not get stuck with it and recognize that the difficulty they are feeling at the moment is temporary.

For the next month, the ace of Wands suggests that you have to figure out how to maximize that opportunity because you'll experience a spark of inspiration, passion, enthusiasm or an idea, you'll have the energy in doing something not just in career-related things but other aspects as well. So this is the month to actually start doing something and taking that first step towards a particular interest.

The third card (four of wands) suggests that by the third month, your subject may have already manifest something from that spark of interest, it also suggests that an individual has prospered from it or made it stable, in short, there'll be some type of success involve or a positive outcome in career, relationship or other aspects.

Example #2: The World, Four of Cups, Six of Wands

Again, you'll have to look at the flow of the cards, so you can check out if there are similarities or none at all, the numbers, the cards, and the overall flow. If there's no repeating aspect to the cards just like this example, it doesn't necessarily mean that there's no pattern – it's just not that obvious. So you have to go back to finding the flow of events for the cards and what they could possibly mean.

For this set, the example will be a query about relationships. The first card pulled for the first month is The World card, the second is the Four of Cups, and the third is the Six of Wands – so if you think about it the pattern is like an up and down sort of thing which can apply to the status of your subject's relationship in the next three months. The relationship starts at the top (The World Card), then it goes downhill (Four of Cups) and climbs up again (Six of Wands). So overall, you can assume that there were aspects of the relationship that's fulfilling as represented by the world card and maybe that relationship became grounded or serious, then at some point they could experience some sort of challenge that pertains to emotions which is represented by the four of cups, your subject may be undergoing some sort of unhappiness in a particular aspect of their relationship, and they may need to figure out what's really going on or perhaps what's causing that feeling of discontentment in order to overcome that downhill flow.

The six of wands represent some success, triumph, and optimism since the number six also means a sense of balance and harmony. It can mean that the relationship has overcome whatever emotional challenge or difficulty that they have experience.

Example #3: Situation Cards, Obstacle Cards, Outcome Cards

In this example, we'll use The Hanged Man, The Lovers, and The Chariot. Now, these cards are all in the Major Arcana, so it means that a situation is of major importance or significant for the individual's spiritual or psychological level. It's not about the physical surroundings or daily life (minor arcana), it's going to represent something that is much profound than that.

- **Situation Card: The Hanged Man**

The Hanged Man is all about the spiritual state or the unconscious state. This card is not about dealing with daily life; it's more of connecting to oneself or on a spiritual level. So if you pulled this card for a situation placement, it could mean that an individual is contemplating, it can also mean a difficult time because the person is not necessarily moving forward or the situation is at a standstill or suspension. This card suggests a period of reflection or that a person should look at things from a different perspective. Your subject may also spiritually need to connect, but he/she is not connecting to a certain thing.

- **Challenge Card: The Lovers**

The Lovers card is associated with passion or spiritually love, where a person connects with someone or something that has a great depth or spiritual meaning. So if you pulled this card for a challenging placement, it could mean that it's related to choices that one needs to make or the crossroads that a person is currently on. The obstacle that is represented by this card is that a person may be lacking clarity or that one must make decisions to move forward.

- **Outcome Card: The Chariot**

The Chariot card is associated with success, triumph, or having control over a situation in order to take oneself to a certain place or goal. This card represents decision making and also pertains to the freedom to use one's will or power to do certain tasks.

So the flow for this set of cards is that an individual is moving from a lack of clarity and not knowing which way to go as represented by the Hanged Man, then making decisions (The Lovers) and finally having that internal will and drive to put something into play to make a progression and move forward as represented by The Chariot card.

Chapter Seven
Card Reversals and Timing

There are various theories about how readers can interpret the meaning of a reversed card, in this section though we'll only brush up on some common meanings of reversed cards. If your client is asking what he/she needs to learn or the challenge that needs to be overcome the reversed cards are in a very strong position because it can show the avenue that your subject can address or change. The timing in tarot cards deals with how your subject should approach a situation, or the kind of timing is on the current reading. The timing will show you how something is going to unfold or what your subject needs to know in terms of going to the next step.

Card Reversals

We'll provide some examples of how you can interpret the meaning of the card when it is drawn or pulled out in a reverse position. Basically, you just have to sort of reverse its meaning or put it in another perspective.

- **Eight of Swords** – this card generally means that a circumstance or perception bind someone and that a person needs to recognize that they can overcome that, so if this card is reversed, it can signify that an individual is breaking through some of the constraints that are imposed upon a person or perhaps oneself. It can also mean freeing oneself from some kind of limiting factors.

- **The Devil Card** – as mentioned previously, it can mean attachment from certain things that aren't healthy or at a person's best interest. So if it's reverse, it can mean that an individual is in a more growing awareness or in a state where an individual wants to be free of a particular attachment.
- **Eight of Wands** – if this card is reverse, it can have issues in terms of moving forward because there could be some issues, delays, or even difficulties.
- **Six of Swords** – once this card is reversed, it could also mean that there'll be delays in moving through a certain situation or leaving the past behind either physically or mentally.

Timing in Tarot Cards

Sometimes in a reading, you may have to deal with what kind of approach your client should do. If you have a reading where your subjects or clients are asking advice on a particular situation they are in, the following examples will show you how to recognize some cards in the tarot deck.

Seven of Pentacles and Knight of Pentacles

Seven of Pentacles is all about having diligence and patience to work hard on something but not being able to reap the rewards right away. So it's a card that will tell you and your subject that something in their life may not be coming into fruition at the moment or any time soon. Knight of Pentacles similarly is a card that denotes stagnation. The Knight of Pentacles does things slowly and is quite methodical compared to the Knight of Swords or Knight of Wands; he will not rush into doing things but if he decides to do things he will do it well and will take his time in doing it.

If these kinds of cards come up, the timing will be slower, probably more methodical, it's something that's going to happen over a period of time, and your client may not necessarily see the rewards of whatever he/she is doing right away, and patience may be required.

The Hanged Man and Four of Swords

Both of these cards denote that quick action and activity is not going to happen. The Hanged Man card can mean that your subject may need to pause or reflect. It can also mean that your subject may not have the energy to do a particular endeavor at this time. It can also mean not being able to move forward and that an individual may need to surrender something to move forward. The Four of Swords is about a period of recuperation, and it mainly denotes a healing phase probably from stress or a broken relationship. So these cards can tell your subject that things may not be moving forward at this time in terms of unfolding events.

The Knight of Swords and Eight of Wands

The Eight of Wands is a card that is looking forward to something; it has some positive element to it and usually denotes a fast pace of progress or being able to move forward. It has a lot of quick energy in it, and some information can also come to you, which will help you accomplish things faster. Knight of Swords is a similarly active card, so if your client asks you how something is going to unfold or the timing of a certain event, once you pull these cards it can mean that something is going to happen very quickly, but of course, there's also some precaution because you might also need to take a step back and not rush too much.

Cards Denoting Transition or New Beginnings

Cards that show transition or change can also be found in the Major Arcana and the minor ones, in this section, you'll learn some of these cards and how they suggest a change or new beginnings in an individual's life.

- **The Death Card** – this card notoriously means that an individual is going through some kind of change and because of that transition; the person will be changed, moved through it and possibly come out a different person either growing or developing in some way.
- **The Tower of Card** – it denotes an abrupt change and may mean that an individual may sometimes need to let go of whatever we are holding to allow a significant change to occur.
- **The Fool Card** – denotes that an individual may need to take a leap of faith, start something fresh or doing something that you haven't done before is required.
- **Six of Swords** – denotes that you need to move through a situation because a better one is ahead. It

can also mean that an individual may need to move to a new location or travel for a change.

For transition cards, your subject may need to recognize that a new start, a new learning or a new approach is required, these things are important in readings that has a position around that particular theme.

Relationship Cards

If you're going to do a reading on relationships, there are a lot of cards in the tarot deck that speaks clearly about relationships. Regardless if a card has a positive connotation or it shows a negative spin or some sort of difficulty as long as it's in the realm of relationships, these cards will have a strong position in a reading.

- **Seven of Cups** – this card in terms of the relationship suggests that there are lots of emotions or desire but an individual may have lots of choices and might not be clear of how they feel or who to choose. It also denotes not having clarity in a relationship.
- **Knight of Cups** – this card can mean the style of a particular relationship and tends to be in a romantic placement.
- **Ten of Cups** – it denotes positivity, a sense of completion and happiness in a certain relationship.
- **The Knight of Pentacles** – it is a very practical earth card that denotes an individual has worked very hard, and in terms of relationship one or both parties are independent and self – sufficient. One or

both parties may not want the kind of relationship that is being too dependent on one another.

- **Five of Swords** – the number five is denoting strife which can signify difficulties in a relationship. It can also mean a lot of competition or struggle.

Chapter Eight
The Meaning of Each Tarot Card

In this chapter, you'll learn the basic meanings of the tarot cards. You don't really need to memorize every meaning or interpretation of each card right away, but you have to know at least its background or the values, ideas, and principles it represents so that you can understand how it could relate to another card or to an aspect of one's life. You'll also get to learn the general meaning of the 'types' of cards found in the deck – they are called the Major Arcana and the Minor Arcana as well as what each suit (Wands, Swords, Pentacles, and Cups) represent.

You may notice that some cards have almost the same meaning or is somewhat related to one another, but as you learn more in the next chapters, you'll soon find out how the message of each card within each suit and its positions could tell a different story or may be interpreted from a different perspective.

The Major and Minor Arcana

THE MAJOR ARCANA

THE FOOL (0)

- A new phase of life begins
- The discovery of talents
- New Experiences

- Risk must be taken
- There's a need to abandon the old and start something
- Personal growth
- New development

THE MAGICIAN (1)

- Possibilities in a person
- New skills are available
- Potential is growing
- Opportunities and adventures unfolding
- Success in everything if a person utilizes his/her skills and talents

THE EMPRESS (2)

- Known as the mother of fertility and growth
- New things about to enter a situation
- There may be a birth coming or a new path in life
- Focuses on marriage, relationship, pregnancy, patience and motherhood

THE EMPEROR (3)

- A need to make something solid or to solidify something
- Focuses on building an idea or something with a firm structure
- Have values of authority, control, and dominance.
- Man of power
- An employer or an authority

THE HIGH PRIESTESS (4)

- A time for reflection
- Allows secrets to be revealed
- Shows potential abundance
- Urges people to pay attention to your dreams and intuition
- This card is all about truly understanding life's possibilities

THE HIEROPHANT (5)

- There's a need for spiritual purpose
- Talks about the search for a personal philosophy
- Encourages a person to increase studying and learning
- Focuses on humility and teachings
- Makes a person get through deeply frightening and hard situations
- This card can sometimes suggest marriage or a serious turn towards religion

THE LOVERS (6)

- A love affair with a trial or choice attached
- This card indicates that these decisions or choices are incredibly important and significant
- One must choose the right path
- A sign of true partnership
- It focuses in choosing intuitively rather than by the use of intellect

THE CHARIOT (7)

- Conflict within
- Struggles and battles
- Potential for victory
- Resolution of fights
- Moving forward
- Overcoming opposition through confidence
- Control and Determination
- It can also mean a journey or change of location

JUSTICE (8)

- Need for clarity of mind
- Impartial judgment
- Requires a balanced intellect
- Legal matters needing attention
- Calls for the fairest decision
- A person is also being called to account for one's actions and will be judged accordingly

THE TEMPERANCE (9)

- Harmony within relationships
- Suggests happy marriage or partnership
- Adaptation and coordination
- Balance
- Patience
- Moderation

THE STRENGTH (10)

- Suggests a person must face the things or the truth in a situation that you have been putting off for too long.
- Overcoming one's fears or doubts
- Courage
- Inner Will
- Optimism

THE HERMIT (11)

- Time for withdrawal
- Promotes silent meditation and solitude
- Patience is needed to confront one's inner world
- Could be someone who likes to or needs to work alone

THE WHEEL OF FORTUNE (12)

- Change in fortune
- New beginnings
- Suggests new chapter in life
- The Wheel makes a new turn
- Remain optimistic
- Someone who has faith that the Universe will take care of the situation

THE HANGED MAN (13)

- A sacrifice must be made to gain something of greater value
- Talks about waiting in order to allow new possibilities to arise

- Vulnerability
- Selflessness
- New Perspectives
- Suggests a willingness to adapt to changing circumstances

DEATH (14)

- Known as the most misunderstood card in the deck
- The end of something which has been lived out
- Suggests transformation or new beginnings will follow
- This card indicates a time of significant change and transition

THE DEVIL (15)

- A confrontation with the inner world
- Facing fears and inhibitions can foster growth
- The Devil reflects actual addictions and dependencies in one's life like alcohol, illegal drugs, toxic relationships, gambling, overspending
- Also, suggest breaking of bad or unhealthy habits or vices

THE TOWER (16)

- Focuses on breaking down existing forms
- Changing false structures and finding true values
- Change around the home
- Emotionally challenging periods in a person's life
- A time of great upheaval

- It symbolizes conflict and overall disruption, but it's for the greater good

THE STAR (17)

- It's about facing things you have been reluctant to deal with
- It could lead to good or bad things, but this action needs to be done

THE MOON (18)

- Fluctuation
- Uncertainty
- Confusion
- Passive
- Suggests of letting go of one's conscious mental blocks
- Encourages a person to allow his/her intuition to guide him/her

THE SUN (19)

- Optimism
- Passive
- Energetic or Vitality
- Abundance
- A time of clear vision
- It is about embracing your destiny and giving it everything you have got.
- Suggests happiness, triumph and good health
- Also relates to achievement

- Sometimes talks about traveling to a warm or tropical climate

JUDGEMENT (20)

- It's a time for reaping the rewards for past actions and reaching conclusions
- Suggests that a person may have assessed and evaluated his/her past experiences and have learned from them
- Rebirth or renewal
- Changes for the better
- Getting well after a long sickness
- Also suggests finding a new career or spiritual path

THE WORLD (21)

- Success
- Achievement
- Attainment
- The realization of a goal or the completion of a cycle
- Can also indicate world travel
- Suggests a feeling of being welcome anywhere you go

THE MINOR ARCANA

WANDS SUIT– wands is related to one's imagination and creativity; it is associated with the element of fire. It also focuses on action and movement and has risk-taking qualities to it as well as confidence, inward passion, and enthusiasm.

Court Cards:

PAGE OF WANDS

- Serves as the instigator
- Curious and restless
- Suggests a creative Spark

KNIGHT OF WANDS

- Adventurer
- Has a youthful enthusiasm
- Has an appetite for risks
- Someone who is in search of challenge and excitement

QUEEN OF WANDS

- Usually motivated and dynamic
- Someone who knows how to multi-task
- She's a heroine and charming but can also be selfish at times

KING OF WANDS

- Has a forceful personality
- Visionary
- Willful
- Reckless
- Extremely creative and inventive
- Sometimes it can also mean that he's not paying attention to details

Pip Cards:

ACE OF WANDS (1)

- Has a lot of creative energy, drive, and vitality
- Has potential for success
- Initiative
- Boundless Energy
- Creative Power and Inspiration

TWO OF WANDS

- Suggests a more intuitive choice
- Two possibilities or duality
- Suggests equally good
- Firm plans should be done
- Envisioning the future
- Readiness for change
- Suggests that a person is standing in his past and future

THREE OF WANDS

- Suggests a stage of initial completion of a creative project
- Ideas are forming
- There are forces of new energy that is being generated
- Readiness to embark on a new adventure
- Taking opportunities
- Can also be about travelling

FOUR OF WANDS

- A time to pause for celebration after hard efforts

- Also suggests that a person should take a break, have a period of rest and learn to relax
- Sometimes it's known as the marriage card
- Harmony in one's home
- Aesthetic pleasures
- Positive connections

FIVE OF WANDS

- A time of struggle
- Challenges will constantly appear
- Expect difficulties ahead
- Open conflict
- Certain issues cause a lot of tension and confusion
- Lacking focus
- Suggests inner conflict or general chaos
- Can also mean that an individual is being pulled in different directions

SIX OF WANDS

- Public recognition
- Promotion
- Recognition for one's work
- Suggest success in any chosen field
- Supportive community

SEVEN OF WANDS

- Stiff competition must now be faced
- A person should hold one's ground
- Renewed determination

- Courage is necessary
- Suggests inner or outer battles
- It can also mean that an individual is prepared for a fight

EIGHT OF WANDS

- It's a card of ease; everything is happening at a fast pace
- There's a real sense of harmony
- Swiftness
- It's a period of fruitful progress after a delay or struggle
- Suggests that everything is in a person's favor but needs to continue pushing forward

NINE OF WANDS

- Strength in reserve can provide enough energy to win the battle
- The energy of a person seems exhausted, but it suggests that one should still move forward to reach completion
- Requires perseverance
- Acknowledges weariness before a resolution can occur

TEN OF WANDS

- There could be a danger implied in taking on more than one can cope with
- Inadequate awareness of one's limitations

- Can also mean that passion can be renewed since a new cycle is coming
- It means a release from the struggle

CUPS SUIT – The cups card is the suit that is related to the element of water. It relates to the inner realm not just pertaining to a person's emotions, but also one's unconscious mind, dreams, and intuition. It can also relate to relationships but in a deeper way.

Court Cards:

PAGE OF CUPS

- Vulnerable
- Introspection
- Emotional Sensitivity

KNIGHT OF CUPS

- Dreamer
- Soft-spoken
- Easy going and gentle
- Sincere

QUEEN OF CUPS

- Emotionally intense
- Can be intuitive and determined
- Can also be jealous and ruthless

KING OF CUPS

- Has a strong and controlling force
- Resists change in an emotional status quo

- One who likes to maintain power especially in relationships

Pip Cards:

ACE OF CUPS (1)

- High feelings and emotion
- New relationships
- Love affair
- The birth of a child
- Self – acceptance
- Spiritual guidance
- Gratitude and compassion

TWO OF CUPS

- Commitment to romance
- Partnership or friendship
- Emotional balance
- There's an attraction of two things or people even if it comes from different natures

THREE OF CUPS

- Suggest a celebration
- A time for rejoicing
- The commitment to a future project or endeavor has been made
- Suggests social life and successful partnerships/groups even from different natures
- Compatibility

FOUR OF CUPS

- Usually, the person is self-absorbed
- An individual is a content with the way things are
- Stability and confinement in terms of emotion
- There's an emotional uncertainty or self – doubt
- Someone who is not sure if they want to make a change
- Inability to make decisions
- Emotionally stuck

FIVE OF CUPS

- Regret over past actions
- Loss or betrayal in love
- Separation
- All is not lost even though it suggests loss
- Suggests that one should recognize what has been lost

SIX OF CUPS

- Past effort may bring present rewards
- Can also mean that an old lover may appear again
- Sentimental time
- Also known as a sibling card
- Mutual enjoyment in partnership

SEVEN OF CUPS

- Focuses on several choices available
- Careful decisions must be made
- Action
- There is a risk of illusion

- You need to avoid escapism protect yourself against unclear thinking
- Also suggests a search for wisdom or oneself
- Emotional confusion
- Self – doubt and can also be about the projection of problems into the outer world and how one should take responsibility for it

EIGHT OF CUPS

- Can mean that a person must leave the past behind
- Letting go of something even if it required much effort
- Suggests of walking away
- Encourages a person to pursue one's dream or ambitions
- Change of relationship status
- Emotional detachment
- Has willingness to walk into the unknown

NINE OF CUPS

- A wish of paramount importance will come true
- Feelings of tremendous joy
- An emotional journey is almost over or will come to fruition
- Contentment

TEN OF CUPS

- Happiness and contentment
- A sense of permanence and future purpose

- It often suggests starting a family
- The sense of harmony
- Also suggests marriage
- Can also indicate responsibilities within a community

SWORDS SUIT– deals with how a person speaks, how one perceives the world, an individual's belief system, how one makes decisions, and understand things. The suit of Swords has the most problematic points in the tarot deck, but it is the nature of air and the mind.

Court Cards:

PAGE OF SWORDS

- Has a quality of wit and carelessness
- Also suggests immature thoughts

KNIGHT OF SWORDS

- Communicator
- Someone who loves to learn and interested in new ideas
- Very expressive or talkative

QUEEN OF SWORDS

- Advocate
- Someone who has high principles
- Doesn't compromise or negotiate
- Someone who is emotional and critical

KING OF SWORDS

- Enforcer
- Someone who upholds the laws or values
- One who leads and decides
- Sometimes unsympathetic

Pip Cards

ACE OF SWORDS (1)

- Inevitable and irrevocable change
- Awakening of mental powers
- Conflict can somehow arise at the start but are ultimately beneficial to the growth of the person
- Also called the sword of polarity or the sword of absolute knowledge
- It's a card of mind empowerment

TWO OF SWORDS

- Stalemate; ambiguity
- Nothing can move or change
- Suggests great tension or deep hostility
- A person must make choices
- Having an inner focus in oneself
- Can also be about denial

THREE OF SWORDS

- Quarrels and conflict
- A period of challenges or flux for relationships
- It also suggests that something sad or painful must be allowed to work something out
- Heartbreak or pain

- Disappointment; delusions
- Also, suggest healing and assessment of the situation

FOUR OF SWORDS

- A need for rest or retreat after stress
- A time for reconciliation after tension
- Recuperation
- Suggests peace despite turmoil
- Postponement of decisions

FIVE OF SWORDS

- Also known as the boundary card
- Indicates contradiction
- Pride must be swallowed
- Limitations must be recognized before further progress can be made
- Suggests that a person must work within the framework of that situation

SIX OF SWORDS

- A card of harmony
- A period of calm after great anxiety
- Release of tension
- A peaceful journey towards smoother waters
- Also, suggest that a person should physically move away from an unpleasant environment
- Indicates physical travel or postponement of decision because the mind is inactive

SEVEN OF SWORDS

- A need for evasion and avoidance of direct confrontation in order to achieve a goal
- One must use his/her logical thinking, tact, and diplomacy instead of aggression
- Avoidance of conflict
- Sometimes known as the card of deceit or secrets
- Sometimes not wanting to face something or someone who hides the truth

EIGHT OF SWORDS

- Fear of moving out of a situation in relationships
- Can also suggest a situation of tension but in this case, the choices are perfectly conscious
- It also talks about how one's perceptions block the will
- There could be a fear of change
- The belief system could get a person stuck which is why the card suggests that an individual must think of something or perceive something in a different way

NINE OF SWORDS

- A time in which the mind is experiencing fears due to bad though
- Nightmares and fantasies trouble the mind of the individual
- Can also mean that the end of the mental struggle is near
- Anxiety and being overwhelmed

- There's a sense of worry and doom

TEN OF SWORDS

- The end of a painful situation or state
- There emerges an ability to see a situation practicality
- A fresh start is expected
- The start of the new cycle is about to begin which brings new hope
- A new horizon is near despite the previous struggles

PENTACLES SUIT – the suit of Pentacles is not just about money or financial matters; it's also about tangible or material things. It's also about the practical and pragmatic side, the stability and security in the physical world. It's also about how one's belief system, spirituality, and creative tendencies play out in one's life.

Court Cards:

PAGE OF PENTACLES

- Apprentice
- Someone who has a plan and undertakes a long term activity
- Indicates new beginnings and a new perspective
- Someone who is earnest and grounded

KNIGHT OF PENTACLES

- Worker
- Someone who is reliable and more mechanical

- Resourceful
- Doesn't move fast and takes his time in doing something
- Someone who exert steady effort to achieve something

QUEEN OF PENTACLES

- Nurturer
- Represents constancy and comfort
- Someone who is self – employed and one who takes charge of their own life
- Calm but not complacent
- Industrious

KING OF PENTACLES

- Entrepreneur
- Somebody who knows how to make money and provides security
- Someone who knows how to build things that will last

Pip Cards:

ACE OF PENTACLES (1)

- Acquisition of material wealth is possible
- A startup financial aid is may be available
- New opportunities that are related to work or home
- New growth in every aspect of one's life (home, health, career)

TWO OF PENTACLES

- There is instability in financial matters
- There'll be optimism and enthusiasm which balances out the anxieties when it comes to financial matters
- Transition
- There could be some sort of instability but not chaotic
- Flexible and can have many options, the key is to be open

THREE OF PENTACLES

- A satisfactory period for a person
- Work completion at the start
- Construction of a basic structure
- Can indicate effective partnerships or collaboration
- Has a firm foundation

FOUR OF PENTACLES

- Danger in overdependence
- Nothing is lost, nothing gained
- Resistance to change
- Focuses on self – preservation or maintaining one's position

FIVE OF PENTACLES

- Financial loss and difficulty
- Loss of luck especially in health
- Loss of self - confidence

- Expectation of failure
- Deprivation mentality
- Can indicate a lack of spiritual connection

SIX OF PENTACLES

- Generous assistance from friend or employer
- Suggest a situation in which there is abundance worth sharing
- Shared resources
- Mutually beneficial

SEVEN OF PENTACLES

- Tough choices need to be made between material wealth and unpredictable opportunities
- Focuses about patience and taking time to make things happen
- There's the availability of options
- Suggests reevaluation and can also indicate a lack of motivation

EIGHT OF PENTACLES

- Beginner coaching or commencing a new endeavor in another field
- Rearrangement or realignment of priorities in any aspect
- One should take a new focus

NINE OF PENTACLES

- A card of unrivaled comfort and satisfaction
- There'll be a reward for industry or material gains

- Confidence in one's abilities
- Someone who celebrates life
- Appreciation for the good thing that is happening in one's life
- Someone who is self - reliant

TEN OF PENTACLES

- Financial security and base for a family
- A new phase in life is about to come
- Denotes values of society, cultural traditions, morals and marriage (something that is unlikely to change or something that is secure)

Court Cards

There are 16 personality cards or commonly known in tarot as the court cards. Court cards have these following characteristics that you need to keep in mind:

- **Court Cards stay true to their element**

They live, breathe, and die in the nature of the suit that they represent. Say for example if a court card shows up, and it belongs to the suit of pentacles, you can expect that this card cares about practicality, it's grounded and deals with the concrete side of any issue since pentacles are of earth elements. The court card belonging to the wands suit represents challenges, creativity, and the self – expressive quality.

- **Court Cards are not gender or age specific**

Court cards express energies, but it doesn't pertain to a certain age or gender. Say, for example, you pulled the Queen of Cups it doesn't necessarily mean that it's about a woman; it could mean that it's about somebody who has characteristics, reactions or experiences related to what the Queen of Cups card is denoting. It can be quite tricky sometimes to not look at the gender or age that is being depicted in the card.

- **Court Cards reflects the level of experience with a certain element**

The Pages card within each suit are the least mature, the Knights are more adventurous, the Queens serve as the channel or vehicles in which the element can be fully expressed, and the Kings are the leaders or masters because it has characteristics that like to have control over the element and sometimes are personally creative with the element. You have to keep in mind though, that there's no such thing as a good card or a bad card, there's no absolute positive or negative card, there could be a positive or negative approach depending on the situation, but there's no card on the deck that is intrinsically good or bad.

- **Court Cards work best if the question is properly phrased**

How you phrase the subject's query or question will give you as a reader a format or context in which the question will be answered. Court cards can mean different things, so instead of just randomly pulling out a card, it's best to have a proper context or determine a certain aspect.

Chapter Nine
Reading a Tarot Card for the Day

The notion of pulling a card every day works best if you really take the time to 'feel' your cards or sit with your tarot deck for at least a couple of minutes every morning so you can sort of feel the energy within these cards. The idea behind this is to focus or become aware of the kind of energy you have for that particular day. It's not necessarily about programming your day or having a planned activity, but it's more of having that sense of both the positive and negative aspects because it can also affect how the cards will show up. This chapter will also cover how to interpret meaning that's "not" in a reading or patterns that aren't obvious.

How to Read a Tarot Card for the Day

For you to be able to interpret a card you pulled for a particular day, you have to pay attention to the different sides of the card and observe the energy you feel for yourself or with other people. Say for example you pulled out a King of Cups card; you can the first layout its literal meaning like this card is someone who is a nurturer, who cares deeply and can be strongly attached to things or people they have a relationship with. Another kind of meaning you could be getting from this card could also pertain to someone who is protective or quite controlling; there could also be an abundance of emotion in general.

You can relate the meanings or characteristics of the card in your experiences throughout the day. Of course, not everyone has the luxury to recap their whole day or record every significant thing that happens (if any), but you have to be aware of things like the energy or characteristics of the card and how it played out its different attributes during the day. You can learn from that so you can have a better understanding of how you can use it in the future whenever you're doing a card reading for the day.

So, basically there's no formula or standard method even for expert tarot readers when it comes to interpreting a card for the day, some books or guides may tell you tips or guiding principles but it's clearly up to you on how you interpret things and relate the energies or events that happened to you with the card you pulled for that particular day, sometimes you just have to be consciously aware of it or maybe do some mental notes. The context doesn't really matter, and according to most tarot readers, the symbols of tarot cards are all parts of our lives' constellations – the more you can define and depict events in your day to day life, the more you'll be able to understand and recognize the energy from a tarot card.

What's Not in the Tarot Reading

When you're doing a reading, one of the first things you should do is to scan the cards and see if the majority of cards are in the major arcana or minor arcana. Below are some examples of a situation that is not in a tarot reading and what it could mean to the interpretation or impact of the message:

Example #1: Major and Minor Arcana (Questions about Spiritual Aspect)

If the cards predominantly belong to the major arcana in a spread, the message is most likely related to a spiritual path of an individual or some kind of growth in an individual's soul. It can also mean an internal processor change in a psychological or spiritual level.

- What's Not in the Reading: The Minor Arcana

Minor Arcana are composed of tarot cards that are relating to everyday life or relating to situations with people as well as how an individual is processing the daily life and the struggles that come along with it. Since the sample spread doesn't have any minor arcana, it simply means that the message is not about your subject's processing in their daily life's circumstances. You can assume that the focus is about the inner growth or mental and spiritual development or connection (if the question is about relationships). Simply put, if there are no minor arcana in your spread, the message is centered on a much deeper or profound level that can affect one's soul or mental growth as well as conscience.

Example #2: Cups Card and Pentacles Card (Questions about Relationships)

One of the most common examples is when your subject asks you questions about relationships. Often times they would like to know the current status of their romantic relationship, and usually, the key indicator in the realm of relationship is a

Water (cups) card because it deals with the emotional element or feelings that one has for another individual. Now, what if a client asks about relationship stuff and they have pulled no cups or water cards? As an example, we'll use the pentacles card.

- What's Not in the Reading: The Cups Card

When there's no cups card in a reading, it doesn't necessarily mean that there's no emotional bond or connection but perhaps the connection for a certain individual is channeled in something that is important, or it's in a different focus of the relationship that's not about sharing emotion. Say for example, your subject pulled pentacles card in a reading, it could mean that the relationship at the given time is centered on grounding areas that are not emotional – it focuses perhaps on a more tangible aspect that the relationship has created like the possessions you bought together or it can also mean that they have a more practical or reliable relationship. Since the pentacles card has an earth (ground bound) element to it, the relationship can also mean that it's sort of a work in progress for both individuals involved.

Example #3: Water Cards (Questions about Career)

If your client asks you about career-related topics, the suits or cards relating to work are usually pentacles (how to manifest it in the physical realm) as well as wands (because it relates to one's drive or passion that one needs to accomplish a goal). So typically the cards you're looking for is a Pentacles or Wands card but what if your client didn't pull any of that and instead pulled out cards like our examples.

So say, for example, your subject pulled out nothing but water cards, you can immediately assume that there's something going on about this individual in an emotional level or they're working through something with a purpose. You can also consider their feelings like if your subject probably feels working in a project that may have an impact on their spiritual or emotional aspect or that particular project may relate to helping others and/or involves creativity.

You also have to think about if there's an emotional basis or drive to feel fulfillment on a particular goal or if your subject may need to adjust their path to fulfill something or monetize something. It may also involve a creative aspect, so you need to think about if your subject is infusing creativity in their work or perhaps they wanted to express more creativity in what they do but may not be able to have that freedom in their current jobs – so you can suggest that they could change jobs to find a more fulfilling career or something like that.

- What's Not in the Reading: The Pentacles and Wands Card

If you or your subject didn't pull any pentacles and/or wands card, as a reader, you have to automatically say to your subject that he/she is focusing on other things or have been dealing with other things not related to work. Perhaps there's some kind of way that they're channeling their career goal through themselves or utilizing themselves that may not be related to a tangible work.

Example #4: Sword Cards (Questions about Career)

Here's another example regarding questions about career. If no pentacle or wand cards showed up and there are only Sword (air) cards on the spread it can mean the following:

- The individual could have a potentially good idea or has a spark of inspiration
- There's some level of truth or information, and the person wants to manifest it but hasn't' done yet
- There's a chance that they might have lots of ideas, but it only stays in their mental sphere and may not have been manifested into tangible results yet
- Since there are no wands in the spread, they may not know how to move a particular thought or idea forward

So if you see a lot of swords in terms of career and there are no pentacles or wands, basically it only tells you that your subject may have an idea that he/she wants to do but can't for some reason. You can advise him/her to maybe just give it a try so the idea can hopefully become real or manifest in the physical world.

Example #5: Masculine and Feminine Cards

There are two polarities – masculine and feminine. Feminine cards (Water/Cups and Earth/Pentacles) have characteristics of being more receptive, introverted, security, stability, don't want to take any risks, and it deals with a more internal world. Masculine cards (Fire/Wands and Air/Swords) on the other hand, are more extroverted cards, active, and more action – oriented.

- What's Not in the Reading: Feminine Cards

If for example, the question is about relationships and you only see masculine cards, you can assume that the emotional or security aspect is not the focus of the message. It can rather have an outgoing aspect to it if you pulled either a sword card or wand card; the relationship could be more direct and perhaps aims to move forward or quickly.

Chapter Ten
Tarot as a Spiritual Doorway

<u>Using the Cards for Creativity, Ritual, and Prayer</u>

Most people are drawn to the Tarot for one reason—to divine the future. And as a divinatory tool, the cards have no true equal. It seems a shame, however, to relegate your decks to Oracle Only status when the beauty and poetry of their landscapes make for such a creative and soul-enticing ride.

I have decks all over the house; I am frequently seen carrying, shuffling, studying, fiddling. The artwork of my various acquisitions serves as a constant source of inspiration and invention; I'm pretty sure this book alone has been good for several dozen gaze-and-ponder sessions. In this chapter, I'm going to offer you ways to work with the cards outside of a psychic reading—and discover all the places you can go with a deck in your hand, even when you don't have any particular destination in mind.

A Cosmic String around Your Finger

A life lived consciously is a magical one. Conscious living is a matter of paying attention —to our thoughts, words, actions, and to the signs and signals from the Universe around us. Miracles and serendipitous events become the norm when you walk in the world with that kind of awareness. One of my favorite ways to cultivate miracle consciousness is using the

Tarot as a daily reminder—choosing one card in the morning as a focal point for the whole day.

Shuffle your deck and pull a single card, asking for guidance, focus, or for whatever your guides want you to know. Put the card somewhere you can see it as you go about your routine—on your altar, the kitchen counter, the table in the entryway where you drop your keys and sort your mail. Then watch not only for the message of the card to unfold throughout the course of your day but also for specific images from that card to show up, quite tangibly.

Draw a Card and Cast a Spell

A Tarot is an indispensable tool for ritual and spell work, as it can heighten one's ability to visualize and emotionally connect to unformed goals and desires. Picturing something into being is a method of manifestation that has been used since the earliest days of our cave-dwelling ancestors; known as sympathetic magic, employing images of the desired object or experience in order to draw it to you is an ancient and powerful form of ritual intent.

Spells and rituals using the Tarot can be as simple or as extravagant as you wish. I have danced the night away in a room aflame with candles and moonlight, around an altar draped with velvet and heaped with flowers, crystals, and twenty-one different Tarot images of the High Priestess. It took me days to come down to Earth from that one!

And I have lit a single, tiny, hand-dipped beeswax taper, studied the image of the Six of Pentacles by its flickering light, and asked Spirit to help me with a medical bill I had no way of paying. Two days later a check arrived in the mail from my insurance company for a claim I had sent in six months prior (and had all but written off because of the time lag) that was, to the dollar, the exact amount I needed to pay the bill.

Because of the transcendent nature of the imagery, the Tarot is a natural for inciting the subconscious to action and stimulating the miracle consciousness required for manifestation. In simpler terms? You have to believe it before you'll see it—and the Tarot can help you create inwardly, on the mental plane, so that what you dream of can manifest outwardly in the physical.

The trick is to choose cards that not only visually depict what you desire but also evoke the strongest emotional response to the wished-for outcome. For instance, the Ace of Pentacles for some might illustrate great wealth and security; for others, a single disk doesn't add up, so the Nine or Ten of Pentacles is their card of choice for a money ritual.

Following are a few of my personal favorite Tarot cards for visualization and ritual intent. I use these cards because I'm so strongly drawn to and affected by their imagery. If you don't have the decks that these specific cards are from, no big deal—I'm only listing them here to use as a reference, if you'd like. Remember, trust your own emotions and instincts first and choose cards from whichever deck or decks spark you the most.

Money: The Six and Nine of Pentacles from the Robin Wood Tarot; the Empress and the Queen of Pentacles from the Hanson-Roberts Tarot; the Sun and Fortune from the Voyager Tarot

Business: The Emperor and the Eight of Pentacles from Robin Wood; the Three and the King of Pentacles from Hanson-Roberts; the Ace of Worlds and the Eight of Crystals from Voyager

Love: The Two of Cups and the Four of Wands from Robin Wood; the Ace of Cups and the Lovers from Hanson-Roberts; the Six of Worlds and the Three of Cups from Voyager

Happiness: The Three of Cups and the Empress from Robin Wood; the Nine and Ten of Cups from Hanson-Roberts; the Ace and Nine of Cups from Voyager

Health: Temperance and the Star from Robin Wood; Strength and the Empress from Hanson-Roberts; the Woman of Worlds and Balance from Voyager.

Personal Power: The High Priestess and Judgment from Robin Wood; the Magician and Justice from Hanson-Roberts; the Woman of Wands and the Woman of Crystals from Voyager

Creativity: The Three of Pentacles and the Page of Cups from Robin Wood; the Sun and the Seven Of Cups from Hanson-Roberts; the Child of Cups and Art from Voyager

Spiritual Connection: The Fool and the Hermit from Robin Wood; the Ace of Swords and the Ace of Rods from Hanson-Roberts; the Ten of Wands and the Universe from Voyager

A single card can direct your subconscious to powerful outcomes; placed in deliberate combinations, the cards, and their imagery can map the story of your greatest desires. Following are three mini rituals you can do, using the Tarot as your point of focus and realization. You can perform these rituals as they are written, or expand on them as you like, such as burning corresponding incense, adding appropriate crystals, flowers, or other symbolic objects, working with the energies of different days or Moon cycles, and of course, casting a magic circle. However you choose to do them, do them with reverence and intent, as you would any sacred act.

An Abundance Spell

Use this spell for increasing your financial income, for meeting a particular financial obligation, or for creating a windfall.

Supplies
1 green candle
Powdered cinnamon
1 Tarot card that represents wealth and financial abundance to you—the Six, Nine, or Ten of Pentacles; the Queen of Pentacles or the Empress if you're a woman; the King of Pentacles or the Emperor if you're a man; or any other card in your deck that invokes the energy of wealth for you
Coins and paper currency, either real or play

Lay the Tarot card face up; surround it with the coins and paper money. Place the green candle at the head of the Tarot card, and light it. Focus on the image of the card, imagining your income increasing easily and joyfully, your bank balances growing effortlessly, your bills paid in full, etc. Spend as much time on this visualization as you can, without your attention wavering. Then sprinkle small pinches of the cinnamon on the candle flame and repeat these words:

Coins of silver, and of gold,
Bring me fortune, wealth untold.
Riches come through every door
To make my money ten times more.

Continue visualizing as long as you can, sprinkling more cinnamon if you desire (the sparks are like magical little fireflies!), then proclaim the spell completely, and thank God, Goddess, or the Universe for answered prayer. Either let the candle burn out or snuff the flame and keep what remains of the candle (wrapped in one of the paper bills and tied with a green or gold cord) on your altar or somewhere sacred until your wish manifests.

A Spell for Love

Use this spell for attracting love to you or for strengthening an existing partnership. This should go without saying, but I'm saying it anyway: Do not do this with energy or intent of manipulating anyone's affections. This is a ritual for divine love, not coercion.

Supplies

2 red or pink candles

1 white candle

Rose petals, fresh or dried

Heart shaped confetti

1 significator card, representing you 1 significator card representing your current partner or the kind of partner you would like to attract

1 Tarot card representing true love—for example, the Ace or Two of Cups, the Four of Wands, the Lovers, etc.

Lay the significator cards side by side, leaving enough space between for a third card; set the love card aside for now. You may place your significator on the left or the right as you wish—if energetic placement feels right, then put the feminine to the left and the masculine to the right; if you want the two characters looking at each other, organize them accordingly; or simply trust your first instincts as to who goes where. (Someone once suggested placing the significator cards according to which side of the bed each person sleeps on. I say, whatever works!) Sprinkle the rose petals and confetti in a circle around the cards, or, if you really want to make an impression, create a heart shape. Place the red/pink candles at the head of the significator cards; place the white candle at the head of the empty space.

Light the red/pink candles. Focus on the cards and visualize yourself and your partner as two strong, independent, healthy, loving individuals, spiritually grounded, happy in your own lives, respectful of yourselves and one another, each desiring a healthy and committed partnership. Take your time with this; make it a physical and emotional realization. Then when you feel ready, place the love card in between, and light the white candle, speaking these words aloud:

Lord and Lady, King and Queen,
Magician, Priestess, love between.
This bond be sacred, two in one,
Heart and soul 'til the time are done.

Now, visualize the kind of relationship you desire, the wonderful experiences you'll share together, the level of intimacy, and connection between you, the spiritual and creative horizons you'll explore. As before, make this as real and emotionally powerful as possible and concentrate for as long as you comfortably can. Then proclaim the spell complete and give thanks for answered prayer; let the candles burn out of their own accord, or snuff the flames and keep what's left of the candles together, wrapped in a red or pink cloth with some of the rose petals, on your altar or somewhere sacred until your wish manifests.

A Transformation Ritual

This little spell is wonderful for any circumstance with which you may be struggling—health issues, financial problems, relationship woes, etc. Healing and release may be just a candle flame away. . . .

Supplies
1 black candle
1 white candle

1 Tarot card representing your challenge, and 1 card representing what you would like the situation to become. Here are a few examples:

Nine of Swords/the Sun (for transforming depression, worry)

Four or Five of Pentacles/Nine of Pentacles (for financial problems)

Five of Pentacles or Ten of Swords/Strength or King of Pentacles (for health issues)

Five of Wands or Cups/Two of Cups or Four of Wands (for relationship troubles)

Eight of Swords, Five of Wands or the Tower/the Star or Temperance (for anxiety, crisis, chronic drama)

Place the black candle on the left with the challenge card below it, face up; the white candle on the right with the card of transformation face down. Light the black candle and focus on the image of the challenge card, thinking about your situation and its energy. Imagine channeling that energy into the candle, infusing the very wax with the problem you're facing. Then, when you're ready, speak these words aloud:

Candle black, candle white
Heal this darkness with your light.
I now release this plight to be
Transformed by love, so I am free.

Now, turn the challenge card face down, deliberately; light the white candle and turn the transformation card face up. Focus on the image of this card, and this time, infuse yourself with the energy—of health, harmony, happiness, prosperity, whatever it is you are wishing for. Imagine the candle flames burning your challenge to cinders and charging you and your desire with vital life force. Make this visualization count; let yourself experience the healing and transformation in your mind, body, and emotions. Stay with it as long as you can; when it feels complete, proclaim the spell as such, and give thanks for answered prayer. Then either let the candles burn out (if you safely can, this is best), or snuff the flames and take what remains of the candles, bind them together with black thread, and bury them in the ground, preferably of your property.

Om and Amen

A spell is really nothing more than a ritualized prayer, with specific actions and accoutrements that correspond to the spoken request. For those times when there's no time to do ritual or spell work, the Tarot can up the ante on your prayer power tenfold. How? Prayer is a concentration; concentration is attention focused on a single object or idea. The Tarot's symbolism sparks not only the intellect but also the emotions, creating the perfect combination of inspiration and intent, all wrapped up in a neat little package.

A client of mine, new to her spiritual path, had no idea how to pray or to whom; a self-described recovering Catholic, she had long ago given up on the conventional idea of God. She did, however, like the idea of angels, and I suggested she try using the card of Temperance as a focus for her efforts. That was five years ago, and she still talks to that card every morning and carries the loving and familiar image in her mind throughout the day.

I have a gorgeous fifty-year-old pine cabinet from Mexico, filled with crystals, seashells, feathers, stars, tiny lamps that burn jewel-colored oils, and many representations of the God and Goddess, some found, some purchased, some gifted to me by people I love. This is the site of years of daily prayer sessions and many an impromptu mini-ritual; when I open the scrollwork doors and light the lamps, I am immediately lifted, held, and graced by the collective energy of every wish and every gratitude ever spoken there. This is my church, and often I will go and simply stand there, soaking in the delicious vibration, much as I imagine people sit in quiet chapels or synagogues, just hanging out at the feet of God.

Inside on the left, near a delicate silver goblet and a Ukrainian Easter egg, is the card of the High Priestess from my first copy of the Robin Wood Tarot. (I am currently on my sixth copy—this deck gets a lot of use in my house!) And to the right, beside a deer antler and an Aztec Sun, is the Magician, her soul mate; these two visually conjure the God and the Goddess for me, as clearly as if they'd stepped straight from the heavens to stand at my side. And when I'm in need of connection, inspiration, comfort, or support, I choose an appropriate card from the deck that resides among the crystals and seashells, and I meditate on its imagery in the lamplight, watched over by my magical guardians.

I also use the Tarot as a meditation tool with my Neuro-Linguistic Programming (NLP) clients. When someone is blocked, unable to manifest or create positive change in their lives, nine times out of ten it's because they have no frame of reference for what they want, and therefore, no ability to visualize their desired outcome. Using the Voyager deck, i'll have my client go through the cards face up, choosing the images that incite the feeling they're going for. Sometimes we'll play with putting their chosen cards in a particular order or pattern; other times, we'll pare the pile down to one or two of the most dramatic representations and spend awhile focusing, discussing, imagining. Then I have my client study the cards in silence for a time, meditating on the imagery, drawing the emotional energy into their bodies with every breath, claiming that energy as their own.

By the time they leave the session, my client has both a visual and an emotional link to their desired future, something I call a barometer —any choice that faces them, any idea that wants pursuing, can be held up to the image to see if it fits energetically. (Would the King of Wands choose this particular career path? If the Hierophant attended tomorrow's board meeting, how would he handle the sales presentation? Does my current relationship fit the landscape of the Three of Cups?) If so, through conscious action toward the choice or idea, coupled with prayer and continued spiritual focus, seen and unseen wheels alike are set in motion that turn dreams into absolute reality.

Chapter Eleven

Bringing All Your Mystic Skills Together to Get the Results That You Want

Interesting Facts, FAQ, and Tips for Tarot Cards

There are a number of interesting facts out there that many people are not aware of. While you are learning all there is to know about Tarot Cards; you might as well take some time to learn these great facts.

In the art of divination, the use of Tarot cards is the most practiced throughout the world. There are some out there that refer to the Tarot cards as The Book of Divination of the Gypsies.

The Tarot cards have been around since the Renaissance and are believed to have started in Northern Italy.

The Tarot cards were brought to Europe by the Gypsies.

Arcana means secret or mystery.

There are thousands of decks of Tarot cards for different interests that are out there.

Tarot cards were first used for telling the future in 1785.

The original use of Tarot cards was as a card game.

There are a number of questions that you might have when it comes to Tarot cards. Here are some of the most common questions.

What is the length of an average reading? The average reading should take about 15 minutes. This is dependent on the depth of the reading.

Does someone have to give me a Tarot card deck for it to work? The simple answer to this question is NO. You will find that some of the best decks you will find are the ones you select for yourself.

Is reading Tarot cards dangerous? The basic answer to this is NO. There is no calling of evil spirits involved in Tarot cards.

Do you have to be psychic to be able to read Tarot cards? The answer to this question is YES. Now keep in mind that everyone out there has a certain level of psychic abilities if they Know how to tap into them.

While there are a number of questions that you can ask the Tarot cards, there are some questions that you should never ever ask the Tarot cards. Here is a list of questions that you should not ask the Tarot cards, as well as the reasons why.

Any question about an ex. You want to make sure that you have positive energies when you are reading cards. Asking questions about someone that you might not have positive emotions about can skew the reading.

Do not ask a question that does not apply to you specifically. You have to ask the Tarot cards about you specifically. You will not be able to get a clear reading for someone that is not in the room.

Specific questions. You can ask generalized questions, but the cards are not going to be able to give your specific names, dates, or times.

Yes or No questions. The Tarot cards are a guide: you want to find more generalized questions that they can map out for you.

When you will die, once again, this is a more specific question than you should not be asking. This is also a question that the Tarot cards just cannot answer. What might be accurate today could change tomorrow depending on if you have made a choice that will change your current path.

Am I pregnant? There are far easier ways to find the answer to this question. Besides, this is a yes or no question and so cannot be asked to the cards.

Now that you have all this information, you might want to look for a few tips and tricks to help you get started on your Tarot card journey. We have put together a few that might help you out as you are starting out.

Learn to phrase the question. You cannot get specific information from the cards, so you will want to know how to ask the questions. For example, you would not ask how many kids you will have. Instead, you would want to phrase the question as what is the potential for having kids.

Do not second-guess yourself. There are too many times that beginners doubt their reading and will do a reading over and over again. This doubt will cloud the cards and skew the results.

Start simple. There are those out there that want to jump with both feet first. This is not the best idea when it comes to Tarot card reading. You want to progress naturally, which means that you need to keep it simple at first until you are more comfortable with what you are doing.

Learn one a day. Draw one card a day and learn everything you can about that card. You might want to keep a journal and put each card in the journal. Generally, you will want to put in how it made you feel, what it means, and later on, you can put what the reverse of the card means. As you progress, you will fill your journal and learn the cards.

The main idea behind Tarot cards is to be able to give a great reading while having a great time. Just keep in mind that the position of the cards as well as if they are right-side up or upside down makes a difference. There are different meanings for each card and in each category. We just wanted you to start with the basics, and then you should be able to expand upon these basics. Only you will know when you are ready to expand.

Every person is different, so the rate of acceleration is different for each person. If you are finding that you are not able to get the concepts right away, it is fine. Some of the greatest tarot card readers out there took years just to understand the basics.

You will simply want to make sure that you understand one concept prior to moving on to something else.

Chapter Twelve
Setting boundaries

While setting boundaries isn't the sexiest topic in the world, it is, in my experience, the most necessary exercise in any magical practice. This is true for many reasons. People are coming for readings in deep vulnerability; they are asking questions and revealing parts of themselves that they oftentimes conceal even from their closest friends. There is a responsibility you hold as a reader to the people coming to you, and the sooner you define your boundaries, the cleaner your practice will be.

When I first started reading tarot, boundaries were a foreign concept to me. I took late night phone calls, confused professional relationships with personal friendships, had no recourse for last minute cancellations, spent unpaid hours responding to e-mails from clients who had follow-up questions, spent a lot of time worrying about what people thought of their readings and feeling guilty if I gave them unwelcome information. Everything i've learned about boundaries over the course of my experience reading tarot is a product of crossing them.

It took time for me to understand boundaries as an act of self-love and self-preservation and something that makes you and the people around you feel safe. No one enjoys feeling like they are getting something out of obligation, and honoring your boundaries builds a trust that allows people to believe when you say yes, you're all in. I believed that if I said no to something that didn't feel right—the last minute booking that would stretch me too thin, an event opportunity at a loud club full of drunk people on Halloween—I would lose something. It was fear-based decision making that did me no favors besides expertise in what not to do. Read on.

Dependence and Attachment

While there is nothing more rewarding than working with repeat clients, it is important to stay conscious of the nature of the attachment being formed. Just because someone asks for reading doesn't mean you need to give it to them, or that it is appropriate at that time. I've had people contact me a week after their last reading asking for another. It is clear, in situations like that, that they either didn't get the answer they wanted or are relying too heavily on the cards to make decisions. Sometimes, people request readings to look into short-term issues that will resolve themselves within days (fight with a partner, a job interview, etc.). I do not offer readings as Band-Aids for panic. To me, it feels exploitative and unethical. I will not capitalize on someone's fear or desperation. There are readers who I love and respect who will do quick reads for people in a pinch, but it does not feel right to me personally. That is my boundary.

Not everyone is happy with me at the moment, but it has built long-term trust with my clients. They know I will not always take their money just because they are willing to give it to me.

Honoring Your Time

Don't get overwhelmed with the idea of charging for readings. You may not be looking to read professionally and therefore, exchanging money for readings is not relevant to you. However, to give a reading is an expenditure of energy, and to give energy without receiving anything in return, forges an imbalance for both the reader and the querist. When starting out, someone offering their time to help you practice may be exchanged enough. However, when you become more comfortable in your ability to give readings, set up some kind of trade with the people coming to you. Money is just energy, and by no means, the only form of currency. The barter system is a beautiful thing. You can trade reading for dinner, a piece of art, a bottle of wine, a massage, and the list goes on.

If you intend to read professionally, it is essential to place a monetary value on your time. Oftentimes clients will e-mail after the reading with one more question or want to follow up on things that came up during the reading. Schedule a follow-up appointment for a pro-rated amount (I offer 15-minute follow-ups) rather than sending a long e-mail or getting on a late night phone call.

It took months of people cancelling appointments at the last minute or not showing up altogether, arguing with me about price and giving follow-up readings for free for me to decide to implement things like a set rate and a cancellation policy. This was scary. Any time we defend our worth—monetary or otherwise—we are probably going to scare the shit out of ourselves a little bit. I already felt like I won the lottery by being able to read tarot professionally and didn't want to push it, but nothing was lost. No one fought me or questioned it. I didn't lose clients or get wiped off the face of the earth. Same story when I raised my rates, cut down on events, and stopped offering in-home readings. Even my fussiest Manhattan clients made the voyage to Brooklyn.

Knowing Your Limitations

The scope of what the tarot can provide a person will never cease to floor me in its expansiveness. The healing and transformation i've seen occur from readings has brought me to tears over and over again. But—and this is a big but—there are indispensable forms of treatment that are not interchangeable with a reading. Chances are you are not a mental health professional. And even if you are, if someone is coming to you for reading and not counsel on their mental health, then stay in your own lane.

Part of honoring the responsibility others entrust in you is to know when to call it. I've had clients come to me supremely fucked up by readers who gave unsolicited and uninformed advice: recovering addicts told that total sobriety wasn't necessary, people with mental illness advised to get off their medication, cancer patients instructed to change their treatment. I have personal thoughts on all of these matters, but a client isn't coming to you for advice, they are coming for channeled, intuitive guidance.

Sometimes, people just need help beyond a reading's capacity. Anything can come up in a reading—mental illness, childhood trauma, sexual abuse, grief, physical ailments—but that does not mean that you personally have the tools to deal with any and all of these matters. I certainly do not. I do, however, have an arsenal of healers whom I trust and refer people to. This includes therapists, body workers, Reiki practitioners, hypnotists, acupuncturists, mediums, breathworkers, yoga instructors, shamans, intuitive, other tarot readers and, yes, doctors and psychiatrists. If someone's needs exceed your ability to meet them, it is useful to have resources on hand for them and important to guide them to the help they need when you cannot give it. An extreme scenario of this is if someone comes in presenting a danger to themselves or others, they should be immediately referred to a physician. Usually, a client will just need ongoing support in continuing their work. Many readers go on to train in additional modalities to provide a more holistic healing experience for their clients and see them through their process.

Self-Care

There is an agreement you make stepping into healership to soften the veil of your ego to feel someone else's experience truly. But once the reading is over, this energy must be released. You are a messenger for the information of the cards; what they deliver to the client is not your fault or your burden. Oftentimes, reading is just the beginning for a person, as it lays out a map of what they need to do in order to reach their highest potential. This is where the aforementioned resources are a valuable way of further supporting your client in the now what?Space they sometimes find themselves in. You diminish your use if you hold on to reading after it is over. Healers have various ways of shaking off excess energy after giving a reading—from prayer and meditation to dancing to taking a bath to go for a walk to watching trashy TV. It doesn't have to be super spiritual; it just has to work for you.

Consent

This one's a biggie, but it is also very simple. If someone doesn't ask for a reading, don't give them one. If you offer someone reading and they don't explicitly say yes, don't give them one. I've had people come for readings pissed off, skeptical, reluctant, insisting that this was all bullshit. But they still came. They travelled to my space to receive a reading. And, despite their hesitation, when I asked if they wanted to move forward with the reading, they said yes. It's easy to get a little over-enthusiastic at the beginning when we are learning the cards and want to offer them to everyone, and that's largely positive. But respecting other people's boundaries is paramount to a practice that is rooted in integrity. Only yes means yes, y'all.

Chapter Thirteen
Tarot Reading FAQ

When giving a reading, what do I do first?

Take some time with the person before jumping in to pull cards for them. Depending on where you are, have your setup ready—the bare minimum of which is two seats with a surface in between to lay the cards out. Think about the best way to make you and the client feel comfortable, whether it is engaging in some chit chat or starting off with a quiet moment. I tend to ask my clients a few innocuous questions at the beginning—where they're coming from, inquiring about something they're wearing, how about this fucking weather, huh?—before jumping into the realness. For returning clients, it's nice to touch base briefly, and for new clients, it aids in snapping them out of any anxiety or awkwardness they may feel coming into a reading.

Do you talk to a client at length before a reading starts? If so, about what?

This is something that you, as the reader, can decide upon beforehand or leave up to your client. I have some people come in, and they won't say a word before we start either because they're skeptical and want to test me or are otherwise unwilling to give details about what's going on. After the aforementioned small talk is over (run time of which is approximately two minutes), I ask if there is anything they want their reading to be focused on or based around, any area or aspect of their life where they feel like they need more clarity or direction. When people come uncertain of what to focus on, I advise them to ask about the matter that is sitting heaviest in their heart. I also let them know reading can be left completely open, and we can begin with a general overview. It is worth noting that a general reading becomes specific very quickly, but that we let the cards decide what to focus on rather than setting the intention beforehand. This is the case one in every five times, with people typically coming for readings aware of what their intention is going into it, and willing to share that with you. I used to be scared of the people who didn't say anything before a reading started, but I have come to prefer that over clients who spend the first twenty minutes of their reading explaining their circumstances in-depth. This is not a therapy session, and getting bogged down in the details of a story is not necessary for you as the reader or helpful for them as the client. If they do want to share information, I try to limit it to five minutes of conversation before drawing cards. I have found this is a healthy balance of starting reading at an appropriate level of depth—you don't have to do the time-wasting guess-work of it seems like this is a love reading but you also don't have too much subjective narrative cluttering your ability to cut to the heart of the matter.

How do I start pulling cards?

After speaking to your client and solidifying the intention, shuffle the cards however you like. I tend to start shuffling the moment I sit down with them, during the chit-chat, and keep going until we're ready to start the reading. Depending on how the conversation goes, this is the point where I decide what spread I will use for their reading. I give them the deck to cut. However, they like, and however many times they like, and then put it back together. I am not particular about this. Some readers have their clients cut the deck three times in a certain direction with their left hand. Sure, why not? Regardless, the deck will not be put back together wrong. When they hand it back to you, take a breath, focus your intention, say a prayer, and pull the damn things.

How will I know when to pull more cards?

Any time you feel like you're about to say uhh or feel a desire to dig deeper into a card's meaning,

Pull another card. Any time it seems like there is something more to a story, pull another card. If something doesn't feel right, pull another card. Don't be precious about this.

How will I know when I am done with the reading?

In a perfect world, every reading ends the same way as good sex—decisively, intuitively, and with both parties feeling satisfied. While my readings have a run time of one hour, I never set a timer for them. Maybe it's magic, maybe it's practice, maybe i've given enough readings to get into a groove of arcing a reading around the length of an hour, but they just seem to end right at the hour mark naturally. For me, a reading ending feels like a door closing, a definitive feeling that all information available to that person to aid them in their intention has been delivered. I leave a small window of time, in the end, to ask them if they have any questions, but this is to follow up on what's already been covered. In less than ideal scenarios, clients will push for more time or open up a completely new topic at the end of a reading. If it can be answered in a couple of cards, I will let it happen. But, if at the fifty-seven-minute mark someone says but what about my family? I let them know this is a subject too complicated to be appropriately assessed in the remaining time. It's not the best feeling in the world, but the client doesn't always have to be happy in order for a reading to be complete. I've painted comprehensive, practical pictures for clients of how to move forward from where they are, and sometimes where they are is such a shitshow that it doesn't look a whole lot better than where they are at the current time. This is okay. You are not a performing monkey. You are not reading tarot to tell people what they want to hear. If you feel like you do not have more information for them, that is how you know the reading is over.

I know you mention that it's hard to be wrong if you are aligned with your intuition, but real talk, what do you do when the person you're reading for says you're wrong?

Alright, my sweet, scared, doe-eyed little peaches. The honest-to-god truth is I don't really know how to answer this question. I waited for this nightmarish moment for years before accepting it probably wouldn't happen. Granted, I don't go into the depth that some mediums and intuitive do.

I'm not going to try to pull your grandmother's name out of thin air or intuit the city your father is from. If this type of energy reading is something you are interested in, this book is not a resource for that and here's why: When giving a reading, I channel information from the highest available energetic source, which actually is not the person I'm reading for. It's their higher self; the spirit-clique, angel squad that reflects a truth greater and truer than a person's immediate perception of it. Specific information and details come in at a denser vibration as they are, really, of no consequence to the message and heart of the matter. However, they can be important if someone is coming in skeptical. Mediums—people who channel the departed—pull information from this more human, slightly heavier energetic layer to offer their clients proof of the living mind, of the person coming through. It can be as specific as a name or a relationship or as vague as a smell, but it will always be something that allows the client to recognize the person trying to communicate with them. I don't like doing mediumship. I find it viscerally invasive and emotionally draining. I will allow it in if it comes through during a reading, but I do not ask for it. I'm saying all this because these are the cold, hard facts that you can be objectively wrong about. I would advise not trying to provide information like this unless it specifically presents itself to your through your intuition. If you're wrong, that's okay. Ask a clarifying question and move on.

What I have experienced is abrasive, obnoxious clients who come in not wanting to hear the truth. One of them came into my apartment with a dog she didn't ask to bring with her, refused to moments of meeting them because she said she was unable to plug into that person's energetic field intuitively.

The best advice I can give you on being wrong in a reading does not differ much from being wrong in life—when you are, correct it and move on. When you're not, trust your integrity, hold your ground, and do not let yourself be bulldozed by assholes.

Chapter Fourteen
Tarot Myths Busted

No one really knows where the Tarot originated, but lots of theories abound.

- It's an ancient Egyptian system of divination
- The Atlanteans were told about it by aliens
- It was part of traditional Kabbalah
- It was invented by Romany Gypsies
- It's part of a complex magical system designed to achieve spiritual enlightenment
- [Insert your own myth here]

The reality is that, although the origins of Tarot are shrouded in mystery, we do know a certain amount about it and it's surprisingly mundane.

The Tarot first appeared sometime between 1420-40 in Northern Italy. Any visitor to Italy will be struck by how much Renaissance Italians loved, including symbolism in everything they do, and this new set of cards was no different. The precursor to our modern-day playing cards, Tarot, or Tarocchi as it was known back then, was originally used for card games, the divinatory aspect added in later, around the late 18th century.

That's it! No scary witchcraft or mysticism involved. It isn't related to any specific religion or tradition, so you can adapt it to your own personal spiritual practices or keep it as a tool, nothing more, nothing less. It works regardless of whether you have religious or spiritual beliefs or are totally atheist.

Despite this, several myths have grown up around Tarot and then insinuated themselves into our contemporary subconscious to the point that these myths alone are enough to put some people off going anywhere near a Tarot deck, which is a pity. It's one thing to decide you don't want to know about your future; it's quite another to decide you don't want to learn about Tarot because of some groundless superstition.

So, here are some of the most common Tarot myths and the reality behind them:

A Tarot is a tool of the devil/inherently evil

As we've already seen, Tarot cards evolved out of a simple game. Nothing evil there.

Tarot cards are printed pieces of card manufactured in a factory (unless you're lucky enough to have a very talented artist friend who can make some for you). Now, we can argue about the evils of industry, but that doesn't make the cards themselves a good or bad thing. They just are.

Any evil you may find in them comes from the reader's intention, not the cards.

You must never buy your own Tarot cards

Utter nonsense! I'm not sure why it would matter who bought your cards, but although my mother bought my first deck for me, I purchased the Rider-Waite deck I still use today, and it's always served me well.

While it's nice to have someone buy you a gift, choosing your own cards has the added advantage that you can select the deck that speaks to you. However you came about your cards, it won't make any difference to the accuracy of your readings.

You must never let anyone else use or touch your cards

If this one was true, it would be difficult for anyone to have a reading. I always get my clients to shuffle the cards if I'm doing an in-person reading since I feel it gives better results.

Sure, it's good to show respect for your tools, so you might not want to let a toddler with jam-streaked fingers rifle through your cards, but the reality is it doesn't matter how many people handle your cards. They'll still work.

You must store your Tarot cards in silk

No, you don't. You can store them however you like. Keeping them wrapped up in something beautiful creates a good impression for your clients, but it doesn't impact on the accuracy of your readings.

You must be psychic to read Tarot cards

While working with the Tarot can help you develop your psychic abilities, you don't need any innate abilities to interpret the cards. You're working with archetypal symbols that speak to our deepest subconscious. Your talent as a Tarot reader comes down to your connection with the images rather than any additional psychism. The cards will tell you everything you need to know. Stick with what you see in the symbols, and you won't go far wrong.

Tarot readings are 100% accurate

Aside from the fact that it's illegal to make claims of accuracy without proof, Tarot readers sometimes get things wrong. Even the best readers make mistakes.

A Tarot reading is a little like looking down the road you're currently traveling if you like your current destination, great! Keep going! If not, change what you're doing to go somewhere else. The whole point of a Tarot reading is to get advice on the best way forward, which might mean changing what you're doing. Once you've switched your course, you've automatically invalidated your reading, which means its predictions may not come true now.

Tarot readings must always be carried out in person

While I personally prefer to do a reading for my clients in person, it really isn't necessary. You can do phone readings and internet readings, and they'll still be just as accurate. The only difference is that you'll have to shuffle the cards on behalf of your client. That's it.

The Death card is a bad omen

It's natural to feel afraid when you get the Death card, but there are far more ominous cards in the deck. The Death card is more about change; the ending of one situation as a new one begins. Death is a natural part of the life cycle, clearing the way for something positive to develop.

While it's true that you could potentially read someone's death in the cards, it's highly unlikely, and even if it did come up, the Death card wouldn't tell you about it.

So, there you have it! A basic history of the Tarot alongside a few myths that should have been consigned to the history books a long time ago.

Chapter Fifteen
Summary...

In this chapter, you'll learn some more techniques on how to prepare yourself and also your cards before making a reading. It's very important that you are prepared not just mentally but also intuitively. All the tips, methods and techniques given in this book will only serve as your literal guide in interpreting the tarot cards but your intuition will ultimately become your "inner guide" to help you learn the true message of the cards that will help improve your clients' lives.

Using Narratives or Storytelling in Tarot Reading

Storytelling using tarot cards could be used as a tool for your imagination to tell a story that can enhance your reading skills and make you more familiar with the energies of your card. It's not about interpreting the literal meaning of the cards, it's more about using the images and symbols of the card and how a story may evolve or unfold once it is drawn. You can pull out three cards to represent the beginning of the story, another three for the middle of the story and three more cards for the conclusion of the story. You can use narratives in tarot reading to practice self – awareness and also be more familiar with your deck; it will also help you as a reader to allow the imagery of the cards to 'talk' to you. It's not about interpretation or discernment; it focuses more on your creative imagination process.

Take the time to work with the cards you draw and then try to determine what kind of story emerges from those cards. Reflect on it and also try to notice if the story is something that is similarly related to what's going on in your life.

As an example, you must set the scene, set the tone, and probably make up some characters for your first three cards since this will serve as the introduction of your story. Then the next set of three cards will serve as the climax of your story – so there's a dilemma or some kind of action to the story. Once you have move through the introduction and the climax, you can begin to formulate a narrative out of it and just let your mind flow without thinking about the meanings of each card, just focus on the image and draw a story from there. The last set of three cards will play out as the final outcome or ending of your narrative.

Narratives or practicing storytelling with your cards tells you as a reader that there's more to tarot card reading, it's not just about answering a query or about getting direct answers or guidance from it. It's a technique to help you broaden your imagination, use your creativity and basically learn more about yourself because that will help you become a much better and effective tarot reader.

Shuffling Your Cards

"To shuffle or not to shuffle?" This is the question most asked by beginners, and it's actually interesting because this is a 'big deal' when it comes to tarot reading since shuffling of cards is a process that happens before a reading, that's why many people are asking if there's actually a significance or if there's an impact to the reading if the cards are shuffled or not. It's sort of a way to prepare your cards for a tarot reading.

There's a lot of ways in which a tarot reader can do a reading and the shuffling or not shuffling of cards depends on what kind of reading is going to be implemented, the kinds of questions that will be asked by the client or the kind of method that will be used by the reader. The notion of how a reader should shuffle a card is related to the kind of layout or spread that you're going to use for a particular reading.

Some experts will tell you to sort of 'cleanse the card' by surrounding it with crystals or some kind of energy stones to clear out the energies from its previous reading so the cards can start anew, this is not required but it depends on you if you believe in that kind of philosophy. Another method you can use if you're doing a relatively simple questioning session or simple methods of layout is to just randomly 'shuffle' the cards on the table, make a pile while these cards are faced down and then let your client draw the card because it makes the subject responsible for the card they get.

Now if you're going to do a Celtic – Cross layout for the cards wherein you have to layout 10 cards and the positions as well as the connections of the cards matter, you can organize your deck by arranging the major arcana cards (0 – 21), followed by the minor cards (ace cards to King) with wands coming first, followed by cups, swords and last is pentacles. This kind of arrangement is only a suggestion; of course you can arrange your deck in which you see fit but that order is based on how the energies come down in the tree of life. Again, it's totally up to you, if you feel that the deck must be arrange in this way or that way for a particular reading or whatnot then it's your call. What's important is you arrange them in a certain way and not just randomly shuffle them since the Celtic – Cross layout is quite a complicated method of reading tarot.

For some readers, they let their clients shuffle and cut the cards in the most comfortable way possible, not like how dealers shuffle cards in the casino sort of thing (although it can be done too) but in a way where they will feel the cards in an intuitive level before stacking them up. Again, there is no exact method of shuffling or preparing your cards; these are merely guidelines of how to do it based from various tarot readers' experiences, at the end of the day it's up to you in finding your own style of doing things.

CONCLUSION

Now it is time to close the topic with a final summary and overview of tarot cards. Hopefully, this book will be a valuable resource for people who would like to have the tarot explained. It covers the known history of the tarot, possible speculation about ancient origins, and the meaning and interpretation of the actual card in the deck.

While the first actual surviving documentation of tarot card use only comes from Europe in about the 1400s, the symbols on the cards are much older. It is believed that the deck of cards traveled into Italy from countries in the Middle or Near East. Some people associate these symbols from the mystical Kabbalah or even the beliefs and practices of ancient Egyptian religions.

However, most scholars are not satisfied that there is any proof that the tarot came from an older society by itself. It is just as likely that later writers, in the late 19th to the early 20th century, assigned meanings from their own knowledge of ancient history to these cards.

However, an important thing to remember is the concept of synchronicity. This was actually developed by a famous psychologist named Carl Jung. It explains how events can happen that are very related in meaning without a causal relationship that is clear to human senses.

This is associated with the expression: There are no coincidences. This is how tarot scholars explain their art.

Shuffling the deck, placing cards in a particular spread, and then selecting interpretations may not be random but influenced by the law of synchronicity.

Human brains are very good at picking up on the meanings of symbols. They may even be better at this than always understanding the meanings or words. It is surely true that these symbols mean the same things to people all over the world, and that is not something that can be said of individual words.

In that way, the Tarot speaks to the reader and the questioner in a way that is relevant but still open to interpretation. The tarot deck, with all of its cards, is only a tool. A hammer or saw does not build a house. Likewise, a reader uses the deck as a tool for divination. In most cases, the quality of the reading depends upon the talent and intuition of the reader and not the deck of cards.

No card is either good or bad. They symbolize qualities, interactions, or events that may influence the questioner. In some cases, the cards could represent the questioner, but they may also draw attention to other people in the questioner's life.

For example, the Fool does not represent stupidity. It represents a carefree life. In some cases, a person who does not worry about the wrong things has good qualities. On the other hand, it could also represent some lack or responsibility or attention to detail that could be harmful. Each card must be taken in its context to be properly interpreted.

Also, tarot is considered a divination art. However, it is a mistake to believe that tarot is only there to predict the future. In fact, even parts of a spread that represent the future only represent a possible future if the present course of action isn't changed. That is why tarot is valuable. It helps the questioner understand what happened in the past, what is happening now, and how these events, relationships, or even attitudes may turn out in the future.

In the end, tarot often brings to light things that the questioner already knew. He or she just could not uncover the answers because of self-deception or because they were buried deep in the unconscious. For most people, using the tarot correctly does require learning about the tarot. However, mostly, it requires learning more about the questioner.

There is also not one best kind of tarot deck. Some are more popular than others. Frankly, some new tarot decks are even sort of silly. However, the cards are only cards. If they have the right symbols, and the reader can interpret those symbols, they work. Even online tarot decks can work. The most important thing is for a potential reader to find the tarot deck that appeals to them and then practices their art.

This brings the book to the topic of practice. Good readers do spend time studying symbols and meanings of tarot cards and tarot card patterns. However, the only way they really become good is by practicing. Great chefs probably own a lot of cookbooks, but they become great chefs by cooking. The same can be said about almost anything, and it is certainly true of tarot.

Now go out and practice. Find the right deck, learn to store and protect it, and begin practicing by performing readers on anybody with a question. It is entirely acceptable to begin by doing readings on the reader. However, some readers find that it is actually easier to perform readings on other people. Everybody knows people with questions. With proper study, honesty, and a willingness to have an open mind, it is possible to use the tarot to provide the right answers!

THANKS FOR READING!

What did you think of, Discover Psychic Tarot Reading, Tarot Card Meanings, Numerology, Astrology and Reveal What The Universe Has In Store for You

I know you could have picked any number of books to read, but you picked this book and for that I am extremely grateful.

I hope that it added at value and quality to your everyday life. If so, it would be really nice if you could share this book with your friends and family by posting to [Facebook](#) and [Twitter](#).

If you enjoyed this book and found some benefit in reading this, I'd like to hear from you and hope that you could take some time to post a review. Your feedback and support will help this author to greatly improve his writing craft for future projects and make this book even better.

I want you, the reader, to know that your review is very important and so, if you'd like to leave a review, all you have to do is click here and away you go. I wish you all the best in your future success!

Thank you and good luck!

Sofia Visconti

CLAIM THIS NOW

Discover the Ancient Healing Power of Reiki, Awaken Your Mind, Body, Spirit and Heal Your Life

Reiki has the power to heal our minds, bodies, and spirits in ways few of us can imagine.

This is applicable to individuals of any age with physical, mental, emotional, or even spiritual problems.

For many years Reiki has been a highly guarded secret but it is intelligent energy, which automatically goes to where it is needed.

Find out more in this complete guide to an ancient healing art to living a happier, healthier, and better life.

A SPIRITUAL START!

Start your week with gratitude, joy, inspiration, and love.

Healing, motivation, inspiration, challenge and guidance straight to your inbox every week!

FIND OUT MORE